To B
With love,
Laura, William,
Martha & Peyton

Christmas 1995

The rich diversity of orchid species in South East Asia has attracted the attention of professional orchidists, amateur and commercial growers and hybridisers worldwide. In the last couple of decades, the orchid industry has made tremendous strides. Singapore has played a leading role in this development.

A key contribution to the birth and growth of the orchid industry is the fruit of the labours of the early orchid breeders. My father, the late Mr. Tan Hoon Siang belonged to this group of orchid pioneers. In 1947, he made a cross between a Bornean species, *Vanda dearei*, and an Indonesian primary hybrid, *Vanda Josephine van Brero*. The resultant hybrid was a striking orchid of unusual hue and quality. Named *Vanda Tan Chay Yan* for my grandfather, the new hybrid focused the attention of the orchid world upon Singapore, and it won a gold medal as well as a First Class Certificate from the Royal Horticultural Society in the UK. Little did my father expect his orchid growing hobby would play such a part in the establishment of today's multi-million dollar orchid industry.

As a boy, I became interested in orchids because of my father. I wish to pay tribute to him and to the fellowship of Singapore orchid breeders, who included pioneers such as Professor R.E. Holttum, John Laycock and Emile Galistan. I wish to thank the Singapore Botanic Gardens, especially its Director, Dr. Tan Wee Kiat who so tirelessly revitalised the orchid programme, and Dr. Yam Tim Wing who authored the book. (They both helped to make the book possible.) I am indeed privileged to be its sponsor and I wish to dedicate it to the memory of my father.

Tan Jiew Hoe

Orchids have played an integral part in the mission of the Singapore Botanic Gardens since its inception. Set in the heart of a region noted for the richness of its orchid flora, the gardens naturally became a centre for the study of orchids and for the dissemination of orchid information and orchid specimens for research purposes. Several of the Gardens' past Directors have been instrumental in developing the orchid industry in the region, as well as elevating the Singapore Botanic Gardens to a position of prominence for its exposition and elucidation of the Orchid Family. This tradition continues. Currently, more than a million visitors annually view the display in the Orchid Enclosure which was first opened to the public in 1955. The congestion due to the popularity of the amenity has led to the development of a new National Orchid Garden that greatly extends the physical size and scope of the current Orchid Enclosure.

The publication of this book is made possible by the generosity of a good friend and staunch supporter of the Gardens, Tan Jiew Hoe. John Tan, as he is known to his friends, is an avid gardener and plant collector who has traversed the tropical forests around the globe in search of horticultural treasures to enhance the gardens of Singapore. He inherited this love of plants from his father, the late Mr. Robert Tan Hoon Siang, who in turn immortalised his father with the creation of the orchid hybrid Vanda Tan Chay Yan. Tan Chay Yan was the first plantation owner in Malaya who heeded the advice of the then Director of the Singapore Botanic Gardens, Henry Ridley, and planted rubber extensively. John therefore represents the third generation in his family with close links to the Gardens.

It is fitting for an orchid to be the national flower of Singapore. Equally apt is the development of a national garden dedicated to orchids. It falls in line for the Singapore Botanic Gardens to produce this book to document the orchid collection and the history of the gardens' orchid programme, and to herald a new era in its orchid endeavour.

Dr. Tan Wee Kiat

ORCHIDS OF THE SINGAPORE BOTANIC GARDENS

by Dr Yam Tim Wing

CONTENTS

FOREWORD	2
PREFACE	6
INTRODUCTION	9
The orchid family in the Singapore context	
HISTORY	15
A brief history of the orchid programme in the Singapore Botanic Gardens	
SPECIES	31
The Gardens' collection of species	
Species of Singapore	
Species of the Asia Pacific	
Species of Africa	
Species of the Americas	
HYBRIDS	97
Establishing a breeding programme	
Vandaceous hybrids	
Dendrobium hybrids	
Other hybrids	
REFERENCES	146
GLOSSARY	147
INDEX	150
ACKNOWLEDGEMENTS	152

Since its establishment in 1859, the Singapore Botanic Gardens has grown to be a centre of excellence for orchid hybridisation and conservation. Today, the Gardens has more than 600 orchid species and 1,500 hybrids in its collection. Many of the hybrids are products of the Gardens' breeding programme. From 1928 to 1994, the Singapore Botanic Gardens bred numerous hybrids and registered some 300 of them. Many of these have been recognised as superior cut flowers for the region's orchid industry, and others have become major stud plants for orchid breeding around the world. The Gardens also takes pride in having one of the world's largest living and herbarium collections of Asian orchid species.

Vandaceous hybrids flower luxuriantly in the Orchid Enclosure of the Singapore Botanic Gardens.

One measure of the success of the orchid programme is in the number of tourists who visit the Orchid Display in the Gardens. In 1993 alone, the Gardens entertained over a million and a half visitors from all over the world. Until today, however, there is no single volume devoted solely to orchids in Singapore, let alone those of the Singapore Botanic Gardens.

Several accounts have been written about the species and hybrids of the region. H. N. Ridley produced three important works about the region's orchid species. *The Orchidaceae and Apostasiaceae of the Malay Peninsula* (Ridley, 1894) listed and described 502 species from 88 genera; in his *Materials for a Flora of the Malayan Peninsula, Vol. 1* (Ridley, 1907), he described more new species and genera; and, in *A Flora of the Malay Peninsula, Vol. 4* (Ridley, 1924), he described 675 species in 108 genera. Years later in 1953, Professor R. E. Holttum wrote *A Revised Flora of the Malayan Peninsula, Vol. 1 Orchids*, which described more than 750 Malayan species in 110 genera. This important work was recently revised in 1992 by Seidenfaden and Wood.

Accounts of hybrids are given annually in the *Malayan Orchid Review*. The only other written account about the region's hybrids was produced by former Gardens' curatorial staff in *Malayan Orchid Hybrids* (Henderson and Addison, 1956; Addison, 1961). Dr.

Teoh Eng Soon's *Orchids of Asia* (Teoh, 1980, 1989) presents an account of species and hybrids throughout the region. Recently, two local publications, *A Guide to the Orchids of Singapore* (Tan and Hew, 1993) and *Orchid Growing in the Tropics* (Elliott, 1993), also give accounts of the common orchids grown in Singapore.

This volume, *Orchids of the Singapore Botanic Gardens*, aims to illustrate the rich orchid collection, both species and hybrids, of the Singapore Botanic Gardens. It contains descriptions of some of the earliest as well as the most recent hybrids created by the Gardens. Since the Gardens' collection is an extensive one, only species and hybrids which are especially noteworthy and historically important have been selected for inclusion. For the serious orchidists, the text aims to recall past achievements and provide an up-to-date record of the hybrids and species. For new enthusiasts, this book documents the history of the orchid programme and reveals the richness and beauty of the orchids on display at the Singapore Botanic Gardens.

Part I of the book gives a historical overview of the orchid programme in the Singapore Botanic Gardens. Since there was a very close collaborative relationship between the Gardens and the orchid community in Singapore, references are made frequently to orchid-related events.

Part II covers the species orchids. All of the orchids illustrated are in alphabetical order for ease of reference. Besides giving the description, mention is made whenever appropriate of some of the more interesting hybrids which have resulted from the species described. Although they may not have been bred by the Gardens, these hybrids are often exhibited in the display.

Holttumara Cochineal, the first hybrid of the genus created by the Singapore Botanic Gardens

Part III describes the breeding of hybrids at the Singapore Botanic Gardens. The hybrid collection is divided into the dominant groups of vandaceous, dendrobium, and other genera. The hybrids illustrated here were either bred or registered by the Singapore Botanic Gardens.

Bare facts about plants can make for dry reading. Therefore, wherever possible, the plants illustrated are related to people, events, other orchids or interesting hybrids. For the sake of the non-specialist reader, the use of technical terms has been kept to a minimum. Where certain technical terms need to be retained, however, for lack of a suitable substitute, the definitions are given later in the glossary.

Phalaenopsis amboinensis

Paphiopedilum barbatum

Dendrobium farmeri

Bulbophyllum lobbii

Bulbophyllum medusae

Dendrobium bigibbum

Bulbophyllum sessile

Ceratostylis retisquama

Arachnis flosaeris var. 'insignis'

The orchid family in the Singapore context

Orchidaceae is the largest family of flowering plants in the world. It is estimated that 20,000 to 25,000, or 10 percent of all species of flowering plants, are orchids. Orchids are extremely variable in form, size and colour. For example, the lip of a slipper orchid, such as tropical *Paphiopedilum*, is modified into a pouch-shaped structure for trapping insect pollinators. On the other hand, in *Coelogyne* and *Luisia*, the lip combines with other floral parts to resemble certain insect pollinators. The insect mistakes the flower for its mate and tries to copulate with it! Pollination is achieved when the pollinia that is stuck to the insect's body from the previous flower rubs off on the stigma of the "mating" plant.

Almost every colour is represented in the flowers of this exciting family — from the extreme dark reddish brown of *Arachnis flosaeris* var. 'insignis', to the fiery orange of *Epidendrum cinnabarinum*, to the sparkling white of *Dendrobium crumenatum*. And the size of an orchid plant varies as well. It can range from the minute Bornean *Bulbophyllum odoardii* to *Grammatophyllum speciosum* which can weigh over one tonne!

The two major groups of orchids, the monopodials and the sympodials, are distinguished by their vegetative structures and growth patterns. The monopodial orchid has a single stem which grows in one direction. It produces new leaves at its growing tip and roots lower down the stem. The apex of the shoot has the potential for unlimited growth. These orchids have no pseudobulbs (or fleshy stems) for storage and are generally found in tropical countries where there are frequent rainfalls. An example of a monopodial orchid is *Vanda* Miss Joaquim, Singapore's national flower.

Sympodial orchids, on the other hand, have many stems and are often able to store food and water in their pseudobulbs. Each stem has a growth limit after which a new stem is produced from the side of the old one. An example of a sympodial orchid is *Dendrobium crumenatum*, commonly known as the pigeon orchid.

A typical orchid has three sepals. These are generally similar in size and shape. Inside the sepals are three petals, one of which is modified in the shape of a lip, or labellum. The lip acts as a platform on which the insect pollinator lands.

Orchid flowers are bisexual, each flower having both male and female sex organs. For most species, the reproductive organs are incorporated

Monopodial orchid plant

Sympodial orchid plant

9

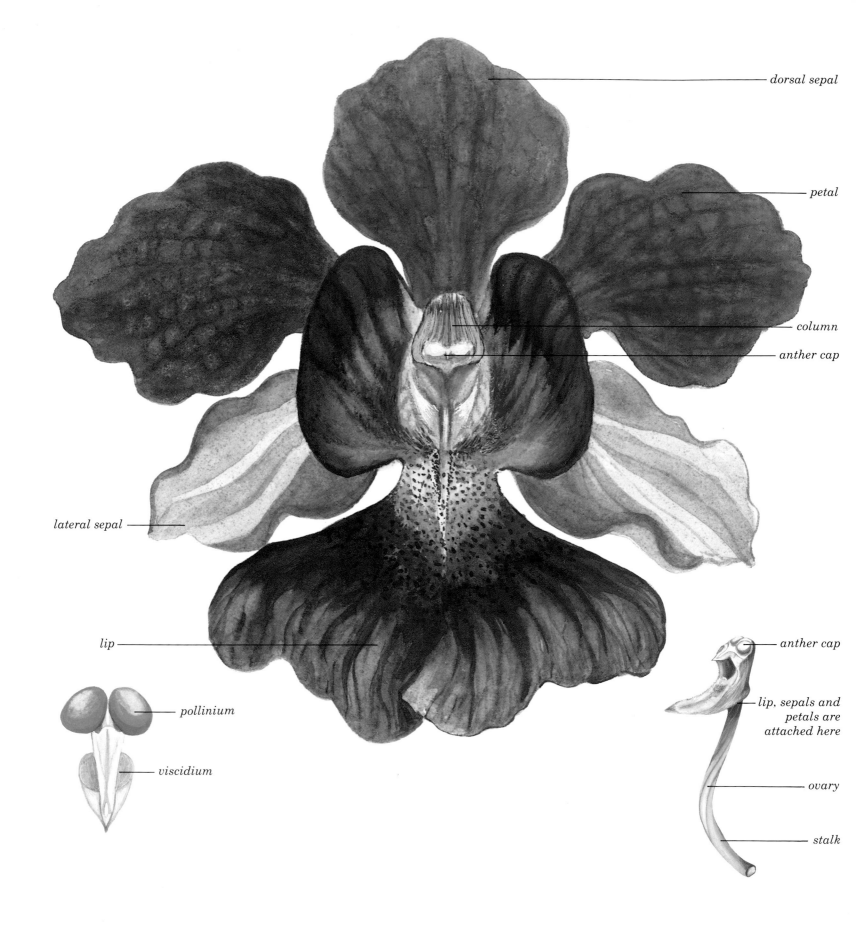

dorsal sepal

petal

column

anther cap

lateral sepal

lip

pollinium

viscidium

anther cap

lip, sepals and petals are attached here

ovary

stalk

into a single structure called the column. The pollen masses, or pollinia, are situated at the apex of the column. The stigma, or the female sexual organ, is situated below the rostellum.

Most orchid species are pollinated by insects. The insect perceives the flower as either a source of food or a mate. When it lands on the flower, it brushes against the pollen cap and the pollinia sticks on the insect's back. When it visits another flower of the same species, the insect brushes against the column and inserts the pollinia into the stigma.

After pollination, fertilisation – that is the fusion of the male and the female gametes – takes place. This results in the formation of seeds. Being the smallest and most numerous in the Plant Kingdom, orchid seeds can be successfully dispersed by wind. Once the seed lands on a substrate, it can germinate only in the presence of a symbiotic fungus. Since orchid seeds are too small to carry necessary food reserves, they need a nutrient supply in order to germinate. After penetrating an orchid seed, the fungus nourishes the seed by its own secretion or nutrients produced externally on digestion. This mutually supportive relationship between orchid and fungus is known as 'mycorrhiza'.

Orchids have developed various kinds of mechanisms to enable them to compete with other plants in a wide range of habitats. For example, some 75% of the world's orchids grow on other plants for support. These are epiphytes found in the tropical and subtropical regions. In order to survive under a variety of environmental conditions, they have acquired many efficient adaptive features. For example, the velamen, a layer (or layers) of dead cells situated on the surface of the roots, is known to function as a sponge to absorb water during wet periods and release it slowly during the dry intervals. The silvery-looking velamen also reflects sunlight so as to protect the roots from excessive heat.

To reduce water loss, some epiphytic orchids have leathery leaves, a thick waxy cuticle and scales to cover the stomata. The stomata only open during the night for gaseous exchange when the air is cool and humid. Furthermore, many of them have pseudobulbs (swollen stems) for water storage.

Terrestrial orchids grow in soil. They comprise some 25% of the total number of species in the family and can be found throughout the world. Unlike the epiphytes, most terrestrial orchids do not need specialised organs for water storage. But some terrestrials shed their leaves during the dry season to reduce water loss. Many terrestrial orchids, especially the saprophytes, rely on symbiotic fungi to supply them with nutrients throughout their life.

Naming of orchids

The name of an orchid consists of two parts, its *genus* and its *epithet*. Using the name of the world's largest orchid species, *Grammatophyllum speciosum*, as an example, *Grammatophyllum* is the genus and *speciosum* is the epithet. The term 'genus' is used by taxonomists to indicate a certain group of orchids which share some common characteristics. Usually there is more than one member in a genus, and each of these members has its own epithet. When the name of a species is written, the genus always begins with a capital letter, whereas the epithet is always written in small letters. Both genus and epithet should be either underlined or italicised. When there are several varieties of one species, the varietal names are italicised if they are naturally occurring varieties; e.g., the alba variety of *Vanda teres* is written as *Vanda teres* var. *alba*.

Hybrids have names, too. Each hybrid has a genus name and a grex (or group) name. All siblings of a hybrid share the same grex name. Like a species name, the genus always begins with a capital letter and so does the grex name, as in the National Flower of Singapore, *Vanda* Miss Joaquim. A hybrid made by using different varieties of the parents is considered a variety of the first registered hybrid. It is given a variety name which begins with a capital letter, placed between two open-inverted commas, after the grex name. For example, the original *Vanda* Miss Joaquim resulted from a cross between two species, *Vanda teres* and *Vanda hookeriana*. Later the cross was repeated by using the 'alba' variety of the two species. The result was a white *Vanda* Miss Joaquim. This white *Vanda* Miss Joaquim was given a variety name 'John Laycock':

Vanda teres var. *alba* x *Vanda hookeriana* var. *alba* = *Vanda* Miss Joaquim 'John Laycock'

Similarly, when a particular orchid plant receives an award, a variety name is given. For example, when the Orchid Society of South East Asia awarded a High Commendation Certificate (H.C.C.) to a particular plant of *Aranda* Majula, a variety name 'Rimau' was given to that plant. Since receiving the award, that particular *Aranda* Majula is now known as *Aranda* Majula 'Rimau'.

If a hybrid is the result of a cross between members of two genera, the hybrid is given a new genus name. Usually the new genus name is made up of parts of the parental genus names. For example, when *Arachnis hookeriana* was crossed with *Vanda tricolor*, the hybrid was named *Aranda* Lucy Laycock. When a hybrid consists of three or more genera, a completely new genus name that is unrelated to the parental genera will be given and the name will end with the three letters

'-ara'. A good example of this cross would be *Mokara*, an artificial genus which consists of three genera: *Arachnis, Vanda,* and *Ascocentrum*.

Each registered hybrid has two named parents. For example, *Arachnis* Ishbel is the progeny of *Arachnis hookeriana* and *Arachnis maingayii*. The relationship between the hybrid and its parents can be expressed in the following way:

Arachnis Ishbel (*Arachnis hookeriana* x
Arachnis maingayii)

This designation shows that *Arachnis* Ishbel is the progeny of *Arachnis hookeriana* and *Arachnis maingayii*. *Arachnis hookeriana*, which is written first, is the female or seed-bearing parent; *Arachnis maingayii*, which appears next, is the male or the pollen-giving parent.

Since the birth of the first orchid hybrid, *Calanthe* Dominyi, in 1856, the world's orchid breeders have produced more than 100,000 registered or named hybrids. After a hybrid is made, the breeder can make known to the world his new creation by submitting a completed registration form to the International Registration Authority for Orchid Hybrids in England. Registration helps to reduce the potential confusion in the naming of plants by giving a unique name to the progeny from two registered parents. Information about the registered orchid hybrid is published in the Sander's List of Orchid Hybrids, now available in electronic form through the RHS Orchid Information System.

The RHS Orchid Information System comes on a compact disk and is designed to provide the orchid registration data in a question and answer format. The hybridist can ask questions about a hybrid's family tree, for example, and the answer will appear on the screen in a matter of seconds.

The Information System has been jointly developed by the Royal Horticultural Society, the American Orchid Society, Singapore Botanic Gardens and a group of Australian computer experts.

Aranda Majula

Above: The Bandstand has been a much-loved landmark for visitors for many years.

Right: Staff of the Gardens in the early 20th century

A brief history of the orchid programme in the Singapore Botanic Gardens

Orchids have been associated with the Singapore Botanic Gardens from the time of its establishment in 1859.

The Gardens' earliest records show that in the mid-1870s, when H. J. Murton was the Superintendent, the Singapore Botanic Gardens began to cultivate orchid species in an Orchid House. Such early associations are not surprising because the diversity and size of the Orchidaceae make it one of the most interesting plant families to collect and study.

In the second half of the 19th century, the Singapore Botanic Gardens became an important source for species acquisition in the region. Regular exchange programmes took place with other botanic institutions throughout the world. Orchids which were native to the region, such as those in the genera *Vanda, Dendrobium* and *Paphiopedilum*, were exchanged for the South American epiphytes such as *Cattleya, Catasetum* and *Oncidium*. The Gardens also exchanged plants with the botanical institutions of the region such as Sri Lanka, India and Indonesia. Consequently, the species collection increased greatly.

Nathaniel Cantley became the Superintendent of the Gardens in 1880. He placed more emphasis on forestry research but continued the orchid exchange activities. When Henry Ridley, a trained orchidologist, became the Director of the Gardens in 1888, he embarked on a concerted programme to develop the orchid collection in terms of its size and quality. In 1889, a new Orchid House was built adjacent to the old one. The new 16 m x 14 m structure contained four parallel walks with staging on either side. The roof was made of roller blinds that could be easily raised or lowered depending on the weather. The orchids liked their new home and bloomed profusely both inside and outside the house. Species that flowered regularly included those in the genera *Cattleya, Dendrobium, Bulbophyllum, Sarcochilus, Eria, Neuwiedia, Apostasia, Bromheadia, Calanthe, Paphiopedilum, Liparis, Nephelaphyllum, Angraecum, Stanhopea, Peristeria, Leptotes, Rodriguezia, Brassia, Oncidium, Podochilus,* and *Arundina.* As the success of the Orchid House grew, more species were introduced from all over the world.

Mr. H. N. Ridley

In order to keep the Orchid House as full of flowering plants as possible, a new orchid nursery was established in the same year. Records showed that a total of 5,000 orchid plants were grown in the nursery. In 1890, over 300 plants of *Phalaenopsis grandiflora* were in bloom at one time.

Ridley travelled extensively throughout the region to collect orchids to enrich the Gardens' living and herbarium collections. At the same time, C. Curtis of the Penang Botanic Gardens, which was under the administration of the Singapore Botanic Gardens, collected species from North Malaysia. The *Gardens Catalogue*, written by J. W. Anderson in 1912, revealed the richness of orchid species in the Gardens at the time. He recorded that the total number of species in the Gardens was 1739, of which 276 were orchids, the largest group in the Gardens. It was followed by 261 ferns, 245 palms, 191 legumes and 170 aroids.

As a result of these efforts, towards the end of Ridley's administration, a large number of orchid species had been cultivated in the Singapore Botanic Gardens. Ridley was also the author of the well known *A Flora of the Malay Peninsula, Vol. 4* (Ridley, 1924) in which he described 675 orchid species in 108 genera. Incidentally, even though Ridley contributed much to furthering our understanding of the region's orchids, he is remembered primarily for introducing the para rubber tree to South East Asia.

An important event in Singapore's orchid history occurred during Ridley's administration. In 1893, while working in her garden in Tanjong Pagar, Agnes Joaquim discovered an orchid which had previously escaped her attention. It was a most beautiful yet unknown flower growing between plants of *Vanda teres* and *Vanda hookeriana*. Fascinated by her discovery, Miss Joaquim immediately took it to Ridley. After comparing the flower with those of *V. teres* and *V. hookeriana*, Ridley realised that the new plant had similarities with the two *Vanda* species and made the suggestion that it was a hybrid between the two species. Subsequently, the plant was registered by Ridley under the name *Vanda* Miss Joaquim, in honour of its founder who was happy to give some plants to the Gardens. From those days, *Vanda* Miss Joaquim has proven to be exceptionally vigorous and free flowering, and it has been observed that the discovery of *Vanda* Miss Joaquim was an important prelude to the development of the region's commercial orchid industry.

In 1912, I. H. Burkill was appointed the Director of the Singapore Botanic Gardens and, like his predecessors, continued to expand the orchid programme. He added many new species to the orchid collection and generally improved the cultural techniques.

The orchid programme in the Singapore Botanic Gardens entered a new era when R. E. Holttum came to Singapore in 1922 as an Assistant Director, the position he held until 1925 when he assumed directorship of the Gardens. Holttum's prime interest was in the taxonomy of ferns. However, he was also extremely enthusiastic about introducing more free-flowering plants for gardens in the tropical lowlands and one obvious choice was the orchid. His vision of producing free-flowering orchid hybrids sprang from observing the prolific habit of *Vanda* Miss Joaquim and this led to his developing a special hybridisation programme.

Although *Calanthe* Dominyi, the first orchid hybrid, was made in 1856 by John Dominy in England, orchid hybridisers had not been able to overcome a major hurdle - which was to increase the efficiency of orchid seed germination. In order to germinate in nature, seeds of most flowering plants have a major food source in the endosperm or the cotyledon. However, orchid seeds, the smallest among all the flowering plants, have no food storage cells. To germinate in nature, they need to associate themselves with specific mycorrhizal fungi and such precise matching posed a difficult problem for breeders.

A visit to Singapore by Professor Hans Burgeff of Wurzburg in 1928 provided the solution to Holttum's problem. Burgeff showed Holttum a new method of asymbiotic orchid seed

Holttum Hall in the Singapore Botanic Gardens, where the orchid seedling culture laboratory was once situated

germination. Developed by Professor Lewis Knudson, the process involved the preparation of sterile culture media which contain all the major and minor elements, sugar and agar. The nutrients and sugar replaced the symbiotic fungus as a source of food supply for the germinating seeds, whereas the agar provided the support for the germinating seeds. Asymbiotic seed germination had many advantages. Firstly, it ensured a high percentage of seed germination

Professor Richard Eric Holttum

Lewis Knudson

John Laycock

in a controlled environment; secondly, it could speed up the growth of seedlings. Hence, this method promised to provide a breakthrough for Holttum's breeding programme.

Excited by the possibilities, Holttum began work and by the end of 1929, he was able to germinate seeds of *Dendrobium crumenatum, Phalaenopsis violacea, Vanda hookeriana, Vanda teres, Spathoglottis plicata, Vanda* Miss Joaquim and one dozen others.

Consider it beginners' luck, if you would. Holttum happened to choose one of the fastest growing and easiest genera to hybridise. *Spathoglottis* Primrose (*Spathoglottis aurea* x *Spathoglottis plicata*), the first hybrid of the Singapore Botanic Gardens' breeding programme, flowered only 27 months after he had made the cross. The plant was very robust and free-flowering, suitable for growing under local climatic conditions. The programme was given an excellent start through the breeding of *Spathoglottis* because the hybrids were vigorous and fast growing.

Encouraged by these early results of his labours, Holttum continued with his ambitious plan to produce free-flowering orchid hybrids for the lowland tropics. He began producing exotic hybrids by making many seemingly random crosses, not only using species within a genus, but also between genera, and his efforts were re-warded with the creation of numerous intra and inter-generic hybrids. One of the bigeneric hybrids was *Aranthera* James Storie (*Arachnis hookeriana* x *Renanthera storiei*). Registered in 1939, it was the earliest intergeneric hybrid created by the Gardens and the first *Aranthera* ever registered. This hybrid became a popular cut-flower for many years.

The year 1936 saw the first flowering of an *Arachnis* hybrid, a cross between *Arachnis hookeriana* and *Arachnis flosaeris*. The cross had been made by John Laycock, an eminent lawyer and orchid hobbyist. Raised in the Botanic Gardens, the hybrid was later named *Arachnis* Maggie Oei. This vigorous plant proved to be extremely free-flowering and the flowers travelled well to many faraway destinations throughout the world. As a result, in the next 30 years, *Arachnis* Maggie Oei dominated the orchid cut-flower market and became the symbol for Singapore orchids.

In 1939, *Oncidium* Goldiana (*Oncidium sphacelatum* x *Oncidium flexuosum*) flowered and has the distinction of being the first *Oncidium* hybrid produced by the Gardens. This hybrid was also known as the Golden Shower or the Dancing Lady orchid. Unfortunately, the Gardens did not register the hybrid because World War II intervened. It was subsequently registered by F. Atherton of Hawaii a year later.

Above left: *Arachnis* Maggie Oei 'Red Ribbon'
Above right: *Arachnis* Maggie Oei 'Yellow Ribbon'

Left: *Oncidium* Goldiana (Golden Shower) – the first *Oncidium* hybrid produced by the Gardens became one of the most important cut flowers exported from Singapore.

Bottom: The first written description of the *Oncidium* Golden Shower appeared in the 1940 edition of the Malayan Orchid Review.

APR. 1940.] *THE MALAYAN ORCHID REVIEW.* 29

ONCIDIUM GOLDEN SHOWER.

(*O. sphacelatum* × *flexuosum*)

By

R. E. HOLTTUM.

THIS hybrid gives promise of being extremely free flowering under Singapore conditions and combines the bright colour of one parent with the size of the other. Though it is not a striking novelty, it is yet likely to be a most useful plant, both for pot displays and for cut flowers; it thus seems well worth naming.

As with most first generation hybrids, this plant is very nearly intermediate between the parent species in most characters. The plants are now (Dec. 1939) at their first flowering, and so have not yet reached their full size. The inflorescences (including stalk) are at present not more than 18 inches long with at most five short side branches but this dimension will probably be considerably exceeded later.

Pseudobulbs are longer than in *O. flexuosum*, with a broader apex than in *O. sphacelatum*. The inflorescences are erect at the base but the apex droops over as in the male parent; the rachis of the inflorescence

Dendrobium Helen Park (*Dendrobium biggibum* x *Dendrobium veratrifolium*), registered in 1940, was the first *Dendrobium* hybrid produced by the Gardens' breeding programme. Five years later, *Aranda* Deborah (*Arachnis hookeriana* x *Vanda lamellata*), named after Holttum's daughter, was registered. It was the Gardens' first *Aranda* and the second in the world. Proving also to be very vigorous and free-flowering, *Aranda* Deborah became one of the major orchid cut flowers exported from Singapore.

The breeding programme initiated by Holttum would not have succeeded without the support of other orchidists and friends. Two who contributed most were John Laycock and Emile Galistan. Laycock travelled extensively to the Celebes, Moluccas, New Guinea, Sri Lanka, Java, Sumatra and

A page from Carr's notes and one of his type specimens

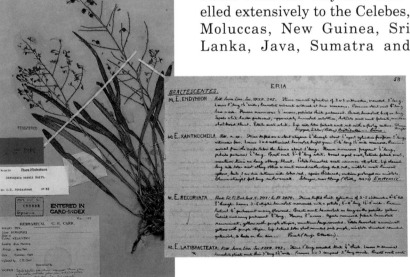

many parts of the world to collect orchids. He returned with numerous plants which he shared generously with the Gardens. The Gardens' Annual Report of 1929 recorded the donation of 300 by Laycock. Galistan owned an extensive collection of orchids and was a master at growing them. He freely shared his knowledge of growing orchids, and the members of the local orchid society benefited from his regular contributions of articles to the *Malayan Orchid Review*, the journal of the Malayan Orchid Society founded in 1931.

Laycock and Galistan were also active in hybridisation. Seeds of their hybrids were sown, and seedlings were raised to flowering by the Gardens. With Holttum's scientific knowledge, plant materials from Laycock, and the green fingers of Galistan, the breeding programme took off swiftly and produced impressive results. Some of the hybrids produced from the collaboration became basic materials for the infant orchid industry in the 50s and 60s. Two examples were *Arachnis* Maggie Oei and *Aranthera* Mohamed Haniff, which were the forerunners of Singapore's thriving cut-flower exports. In addition, Holttum, Laycock and Galistan were also founding members of the Malayan Orchid Society, now known as the Orchid Society of South East Asia.

Another orchidist who contributed plants to the Botanic Gardens was

C.E. Carr. During Holttum's administration, Carr, a rubber estate manager with a keen interest in orchids, made many study and collection trips to various parts of the Malayan Peninsula, Borneo and New Zealand. The Gardens had an extremely good mutual working relationship with Carr, providing him with herbarium services and sorting and distributing his collection, especially those from New Guinea. In return, he donated numerous herbarium samples and specimens to the Gardens. After his sudden death, the Gardens purchased Carr's species collection which included 4300 dried and spirited samples accompanied by his detailed notes. These specimens form an important reference collection for orchid taxonomists throughout the world.

After his initial success with hybridisation, Holttum realised that further improvements could be made on free-flowering cut-flower hybrids in terms of colour, texture, form and growth rate. Hence, the objectives of the breeding programme became more specific. Instead of focusing on free-flowering hybrid plants for gardens, the emphasis shifted to the production of cut-flower hybrids for commercial cultivation. As a result, hybrids such as *Aranda* Deborah, *Aranda* Hilda Galistan, *Spathoglottis* Primrose, and *Dendrobium* Tan Chye Siam were made and became either successful parent plants for hybridisation or cultivated cut-flowers for export.

Holttum registered 28 hybrids during his 27 years in the Singapore Botanic Gardens — 6 spathoglottis, 9 dendrobiums and 13 vandaceous hybrids, many of which were primary hybrids between two parent species. Unfortunately, numerous hybrids raised and flowered during his time were not registered after his retirement. Meanwhile, hybrids produced by the breeding programme began to gain recognition internationally as well as regionally.

Apart from his role in pioneering the orchid breeding programme, Holttum also contributed to the orchidology of the region by writing numerous articles in the *Malayan Orchid Review*, many international journals, and most importantly, a revised *Flora of the Malayan Peninsula, Vol. 1 Orchids* (also known as the *Orchids of Malaya*), in which he described more than 750 Malayan species in 110 genera (Holttum, 1953).

During World War II, when Japanese forces occupied Singapore from 1942 to 1945, Holttum was retained in the Gardens to supervise the local staff. Re-

Holttum's seedling laboratory

Mr Tan Chay Yan (above), the father of Tan Hoon Siang, an orchid enthusiast who contributed seeds of *Vanda* Tan Chay Yan to the Gardens

stricted by a lack of resources for horticultural work and being freed from most administrative duties, Holttum began work on the *Orchids of Malaya*. This monumental work, published later in 1953, is a landmark, the most significant work in orchidology of the region even today, and its success is attributed to Holttum's style of presentation — technical, yet accessible to a lay audience. After the introductory chapters which present basic information for beginners, the *Orchids of Malaya* provides a logical key and description of more than 750 Malayan orchid species. For those of us who use the *Orchids of Malaya* regularly, one can see how comprehensive and user-friendly it is.

In 1949, M. R. Henderson was appointed Director of the Singapore Botanic Gardens after Holttum retired to become the first Chairman of the Department of Botany in the newly founded University of Malaya. During his five-year tenure, Henderson continued to build upon the firm foundation established by Holttum and his predecessors. The breeding programme rapidly gained momentum and resulted in an exponential increase in the number of hybrids raised in the Gardens, many of which were made in Holttum's time but flowered during

Henderson's administration.

During Henderson's term of service, a total of 25 hybrids were registered — 16 vandaceous, 8 dendrobiums and 1 spathoglottis hybrids. Some of the more outstanding plants were the first *Arachnis* hybrid registered by the Singapore Botanic Gardens, *Arachnis* Ishbel, *Arachnopsis* Eric Holttum, *Aranda* Peter Ewart, *Dendrobium* Parkstance, *Dendrobium* Champagne, *Dendrobium* Lim Chong Min, *Vanda* Prolific, *Vanda* Norbert Alphonso, *Vanda* Ruby Prince, and the beautiful blue *Vanda* Jean Kinloch Smith.

A few important events occurred during that time. In 1951, the orchid section was extended considerably by the addition of more beds for growing *Vanda, Arachnis* and *Aranda*. Henderson also built several simple orchid houses to accommodate the increasing number of orchid seedlings. A year later, *Vanda* Tan Chay Yan flowered in the Gardens. Earlier, seeds of this cross were presented to the Gardens by Tan Hoon Siang and the first seedlings flowered in the Gardens under the care of Tan Siew Kuah. This beautiful hybrid (see cover photo) was awarded a First Class Certificate (FCC) in the Chelsea Flower Show in England in 1954 and is responsible for firmly establishing Singapore on the world orchid map. Even today, *Vanda* Tan Chay Yan is still considered one of the most outstanding hybrids ever produced in Singapore.

As Director of the Gardens, J. W. Purseglove (1954-1957) continued with the work of the orchid programme, the highlight of which was the completion of the Orchid Enclosure in 1955. Initiated during Henderson's administration, the Enclosure was designed to display to full glory the unique hybrids produced by the Gardens as well as to promote orchid cultivation. Consequently, orchids became a symbol and an ambassador, not only of the Botanic Gardens, but also of Singapore.

As the Singapore orchids gained fame, it became obvious that they should be used as agents to promote goodwill and closer ties between nations. The Gardens began to name new hybrids after VIPs and visiting celebrities, both within and outside Singapore. In 1956, the first VIP orchid *Aranthera* Anne Black was named after Lady Black, wife of the former Governor of Singapore, Sir Robert Black. To date, the Singapore Botanic Gardens has named over 75 VIP orchids.

A total of 23 hybrids were registered during Purseglove's four years of service. Some outstanding ones included *Aranda* Freckles, *Aranda* Belzonica, *Dendrobium* Mustard, *Vanda* Rubella and *Vanda* Memoria Alex Donald.

During the administration of H. M. Burkill (1957-1969), the Gardens registered 107 hybrids comprising 69 vandaceous, 35 dendrobiums, one paphiopedilum, one cymbidium and

VIP visitors to the Gardens include Prince Norodom Sihanouk of Cambodia (top), Queen Elizabeth II of England (centre), and the then Prince Akihito and Princess Michiko of Japan (bottom).

one brassidium hybrid. Among these were well-known ones used for cut flowers, landscaping and stud plants. Some good examples were *Ridleyara* Fascad, the world's first trigeneric hybrid involving *Arachnis, Trichoglottis* and *Vanda; Holttumara* Cochineal, the world's first *Holttumara* which is crossed between *Arachnis, Vanda* and *Renanthera; Aranda* Lily Chong; *Aranda* Majula; *Aranda* Adam Malik; *Aranda* Eric Mekie; *Vanda* Sanada Kuma; *Vanda* Bellasan; *Paphiopedilum* Shireen; and *Renantanda* Jane McNeill.

In the late 1950s and early 60s, Singapore gradually began winning recognition as a centre of excellence for orchid breeding and cultivation. In 1964, Singapore hosted the 4th World Orchid Conference, a triennial event described by the media as 'The Olympics of Orchids'. Opened by Singapore's first President, Yusof Ishak, the Conference attracted a total of 670 delegates from around the world. Many world-renowned speakers such as Oscar M. Kirsch, H. Kamemoto, Rapee Sagarik, and J. S. L. Gilmour shared their experience on breeding, cultivation, and taxonomy. Several local authorities, such as R. E. Holttum, Tan Hoon Siang, A. G. Alphonso, and Gracia Lewis, also presented their findings. One of the chief benefits of the Conference was to give the orchids and orchid expertise of Singapore greater exposure around the globe.

From 1970 to 1980, when Singapore was intent on building a Garden City, the Singapore Botanic Gardens changed its mission from horticultural and taxonomical research to providing horticultural skills and resources towards helping the nation achieve its goals. Nevertheless, the orchid programme continued but with a different emphasis. Owing to the destruction of natural habitats, many wild orchids were seriously endangered. In response, the Gardens under the leadership of A.G. Alphonso began to channel more effort into conservation. Besides growing lowland species in the nursery, the Gardens constructed the first Temperate House (also known as Cold House) to accommodate the cool-growing species from higher altitudes and temperate regions.

As for the breeding programme, the Botanic Gardens - after leading orchid hybridisation in Singapore for over 30 years - began to share the responsibilities of creating new hybrids with local breeders. Soon, these breeders, confident of their knowledge and abilities, began to dominate the scene by producing several outstanding cut-flower hybrids. *Dendrobium* Tay Swee Keng, *Aranda* Noorah Alsagoff and *Aranda* How Yee Peng were amongst the more famous household names which provided some of the major cut flowers for the blooming orchid industry. Towards the end of the 70s and the beginning of the 80s, exports of orchids reached

S$13 to S$16 million annually.

While the private breeders took the lead in developing hybrids for cut-flower purposes, the Gardens continued to breed hybrids for landscaping, horticultural shows, and the nation's VIP orchid naming programme. Notable plants registered during that period included *Aeridovanda* Jehan El Sadat, *Dendrobium* Michiko, *Dendrobium* Elizabeth, *Dendrobium* Rahah, *Dendrobium* Sirima Bandaranaike, *Renantanda* Akihito, *Renantanda* Hannelore Schmidt and *Renanthopsis* Margaret. The Singapore Botanic Gardens also established a micro-propagation unit to mass propagate popular cut-flower hybrids to cater for the orchid industry. The unit has since propagated many new hybrids by tissue culture.

During the early 1980s, with the arrival of Dr. Tan Wee Kiat, the orchid programme - which had been in a state of suspension - took a new lease of life. An expert in the field of orchid taxonomy and breeding, Dr. Tan returned to Singapore from Marie Selby Botanical Gardens in Sarasota, Florida where he served as the Gardens' Assistant Director, as well as the Director of the Orchid Identification Centre and Director of the Museum of Botany and the Arts.

Responding to the constant demand for new varieties, the Orchid Programme of the Singapore Botanic Gardens once again geared itself towards

Dendrobium
Tay Swee Keng

the breeding of cut-flower hybrids for the orchid industry. Spear-headed by Dr. Tan, the programme produced several promising hybrids for cut-flower production, such as *Dendrobium* Singa Mas and *Dendrobium* Singa Star. A number of other interesting hybrids include *Renanthera* Rattanakosin, *Dendrobium* Singa Hyogo, *Dendrobium* Corazon Aquino, *Dendrobium* Khunying Boonruen, *Dendrobium* Margaret Thatcher, *Dendrobium* Saleha and *Dendrobium* National Parks. The Gardens acquired many stud plants as breeding stock and new species were added to the collection.

In 1990, Dr. Tan led the Singapore Botanic Gardens into a new phase with the establishment of the National Parks Board. The Board was formed to look after the development, management and promotion of Singapore's natural and cultural heritage in the Singapore Botanic Gardens, Fort Canning Park and the Nature Reserves.

As part of the Board's effort to establish the Gardens as one of the world's most significant equatorial botanic gardens, an ambitious 2.2-hectare National Orchid Garden is constructed in the central core of the Gardens. Planned as the most extensive and comprehensive permanent exposition of orchid culture in Asia, the orchids here are displayed on a naturally landscaped, gently sloping hillside, to create a memorable experience for visitors. Species are kept in an Orchidarium.

Aranda Noorah Alsagoff

Meanwhile, the breeding programme continues to produce quality hybrids for a specialist market of cut flowers, landscaping, and potted plants. In the period from 1990 to 1994, some 40 hybrids have been registered; and some of the more prominent ones are *Dendrobium* De Klerk, *Dendrobium* Masako Kotaishi Hidenka, *Renanthopsis* Dhanabalan, *Renantanda* Mary Robinson and *Renantanda* Keating.

In 1993, the Singapore Botanic Gardens celebrated the 100th birthday of *Vanda* Miss Joaquim, the National Flower of Singapore. As mentioned earlier, it was this first natural hybrid of Singapore which inspired Holttum to begin the orchid breeding programme in the Singapore Botanic Gardens. In order to commemorate the occasion, a new hybrid *Vanda* Singa Joaquim Centenary was named. It is the progeny of a cross between two well-known plants - *Vanda* Josephine van Brero and *Vanda* Miss Joaquim.

The orchid collection of the Singapore Botanic Gardens is known not only for its hybrids but also for its species, which are mainly acquired through collection trips, exchange programmes, and donations. Over the years, staff from the Gardens have made regular trips to collect species from around the world, with the majority of the journeys concentrated within the region. Exchange programmes with other botanical institutions and occasional donations from private collectors and growers have also enriched the collection.

Within the South East Asia collection are some 60 native orchids of Singapore and many species from Indochina, Peninsular Malaysia, Borneo, Java and Sumatra. The Gardens also takes pride in having an excellent collection of spatulata dendrobium species from Papua New Guinea and its neighbouring islands. Many species from tropical America, China, Japan, India and Africa also grow well in Singapore's tropical lowland climate.

The present orchid species collection comprises many genera. *Dendrobium* is the largest genus here, followed by the vandaceous genera, such as *Arachnis, Vanda, Renanthera* and *Phalaenopsis*. There are also numerous species from the genera *Bulbophyllum, Paphiopedilum,* and *Oncidium*. Other interesting genera include *Arundina, Spathoglottis, Cymbidium, Catasetum, Cattleya* and *Vanilla*.

In order to grow orchids from the tropic's higher altitudes as well as those from temperate zones, a Cold House, also known as the Temperate House, was built in 1972. It proved to be very successful as many cool growing species flowered here for the first time. Research carried out in the Temperate House was useful in building an understanding of the important relationship between temperature and flower induction in the tropics. A new Cold House had to be built to replace the old one with construction works to make way for the National Orchid Garden. Many new species from various parts of the world have been introduced and are growing well there.

The past 65 years of breeding in the Singapore Botanic Gardens has produced numerous beautiful hybrids. As the Gardens' Orchid Programme en-

ters the 21st Century, attention is being focused on improving the colour and quality of the hybrids and breeding potted-plant orchids for apartment dwellers. Results will be achieved by experimenting with new genetic materials through conven-

Vanda Singa Joaquim Centenary

tional breeding and state-of-the-art biotechnology techniques. A more extensive species exchange programme will be established to conserve both native and regional orchids. In order to preserve biodiversity, artificially propagated seedlings will be sent to other botanic institutions throughout the world in exchange for other species. A pollen bank will also be set up, and pollen will be refrigerated to increase longevity. The stored pollen can then be used for breeding, research and conservation. Upon the completion of the 2.2-hectare National Orchid Garden in 1995, supported by an intensive breeding and research programme, the Singapore Botanic Gardens will become the premier botanic institution for the exposition of orchids in the tropics.

In the early days when photography was just an exciting hobby, botanists had to depend on specialist illustrators to make detailed drawings of specimens for record-keeping. Because of its long history, the Singapore Botanic Gardens has acquired an extensive collection of such illustrations which have themselves become works of art and a valuable part of the Gardens' heritage.

Clockwise from top left-hand corner: *Coelogyne flexuosa, Bulbophyllum blumei, Habenaria carnea, Ascocentrum miniatum, Anoectochilus geniculatus, Dendrobium lankaviense, Arundina graminifolia, Bulbophyllum patens, Coelogyne tomentosa, Bulbophyllum auratum, Bulbophyllum grandiflorum.*

Negri Sembilan, Jirnah river
1923

Anoectochilus geniculatus

180

Dendrobium
Sankauria
from
Chas. Geo. De. Alwis.

RF

The Gardens' collection of species

The rich diversity of the collection - some 600 species in the nursery, the largest number of species of all the plant families in the Singapore Botanic Gardens – is a result of many years of diligent collection and exchange programmes with other botanical institutions. The Gardens makes frequent trips throughout the region to gather live, as well as herbarium, specimens. Towards the end of the last century, Henry Ridley collected extensively throughout the region, and during Holttum's time many valuable materials were also gathered from his collection trips. Orchid enthusiasts Carr, Laycock and Galistan also collected regularly from many parts of the world, generously contributing a large number of species to the Gardens. A lively exchange programme conducted over a century with other botanical institutions in India, Africa, the Americas and many parts of South East Asia has resulted in further enriching the number of orchid species in the Gardens.

Orchid species are collected for several purposes. In the beginning, orchids were collected as part of the Gardens' programme to study the plant life of the region. But as more interesting and showy species were acquired, they were displayed and soon became popular garden plants. After the breeding programme started in the late 1920s, species were also collected as breeding stock.

At last count, the Singapore Botanic Gardens had a total of 119 genera comprising 597 species which have been identified. Numerous specimens still need to be verified, because they have yet to flower. Representatives from all five of the currently recognised subfamilies of Orchidaceae can be found in the collection, for example, *Neuwiedia* of the subfamily Apostasioideae; *Paphiopedilum* and *Cypripedium* of Cypripedioideae; *Anoectochilus, Goodyera, Corymborkis* of Spiranthoideae; *Habenaria* and *Pectilis* of Orchidoideae; and *Arundina, Coelogyne, Liparis, Epidendrum* and *Vanda* of Epidendroideae.

Geographical distribution

Most species in the Gardens' collection originate from the tropical and subtropical regions of the world, with the majority coming from South East Asia (see map on page 33). Thailand is represented by 198 species; Peninsular Malaysia, 186 species; the Philippines, 176 species; from Java, Sumatra, Sulawesi, Moluccas and the neighbouring islands, 173 species; Borneo, 165

Opposite page: A spectacular field of *Arundina graminifolia* flourishes in a secluded part of the island's Nature Reserves. Below: Species of *Paphiopedilum*

species. Myanmar and Indochina are represented by 106 and 136 species, respectively. From the Southwest Pacific region, 59 species originate from Papua New Guinea and 10 from Australia. The number of species from the northern and western regions are much fewer. For example, there are only 82 species from India, 61 from China and 15 from Africa and Madagascar. Finally, the Americas are represented by 103 species.

Life forms

In life form terms, orchids can be classified into three main groups - epiphytes, terrestrials and climbers. It is interesting to note that the majority (81%) of the species in the Gardens are epiphytes, whilst 18% are terrestrials and only less than 1% are climbers.

Right: *Bulbophyllum vaginatum* is a common epiphyte in this region. Below: A clump of *Nephelaphyllum pulchrum* grows on the forest floor.

Epiphytes grow on other plants for support and the term is often used loosely to include plants which grow on rocks and cliffs (the correct term for them should be lithophytes). Epiphytes make up about 75% of the orchid species and are limited to tropical and subtropical regions. In tropical rain forests, the majority of the orchid species are epiphytes. An example of an epiphytic genus is

the region's *Dendrobium,* the largest genus in our collection; next are the vandaceous species from genera such as *Arachnis, Vanda, Trichoglottis* and *Phalaenopsis.*

Other genera which are also well represented are *Eria, Bulbophyllum* and *Coelogyne.* From Central and South America are the dancing lady *Oncidium,* the brilliantly coloured *Epidendrum,* and the interesting *Catasetum.* Africa and Madagascar are represented by *Angraecum, Ansellia* and one species of *Bulbophyllum.*

Terrestrial orchids grow in various soils. They are fewer in number, comprising some 25% of the total number of species in the family. However, they can be found not only in the tropical and subtropical regions, but in temperate zones as well. Examples of terrestrials are the Asian slipper orchid, *Paphiopedilum,* and its counterpart in South America, *Phragmipedium, Spathoglottis,* the bamboo orchid *Arundina, Calanthe, Eulophia,* the spectacular *Habenaria,* the beautiful jewel orchids *Anoectochilus* and *Goodyera,* some *Cymbidium* species from Northern China and numerous others.

Climbers are very similar to the monopodial vandaceous orchids except that an adventitious root can be found at each node. The primary function of these roots is for anchorage, and roots that are closest to the ground branch profusely as they enter the substrata. Some examples of climbers in the Gardens' collection are *Vanilla* and *Coelogyne*.

REGION	NO. OF SPECIES
Thailand	198
Peninsular Malaysia	186
Philippines	176
Java, Sumatra, Sulawesi and Moluccas	173
Borneo	165
Indochina	136
Myanmar	106
Americas[1]	103
China	61
Singapore	60
South West Pacific Islands[2]	49
India	82
Papua New Guinea	59
Japan, Korea, Taiwan	20
Africa and Madagascar	15
Australia	10

Number of species from different parts of the world in the Singapore Botanic Gardens' collection.

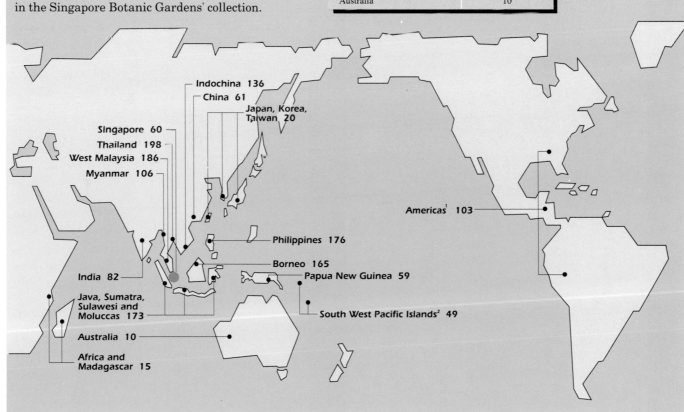

[1] *North, Central and South America, and the West Indies.*
[2] *Solomon Islands, New Caledonia, Fiji, Tonga, Samoa and the neighbouring islands.*

For the past thirty years, the Gardens has provided a temperate house environment to accommodate orchids that grow in the temperate regions and at higher altitudes. Temperature and light intensity are regulated to simulate the environmental conditions of the natural habitats of these orchids. Among the cool climate species growing here are *Cymbidium, Paphiopedilum, Cypripedium, Masdevallia, Oncidium, Miltonia,* and many jewel orchids.

Conservation

It is a well-known fact that orchid species are seriously endangered throughout the world due to habitat destruction and over-collection. If the situation continues, many valuable species will be lost in the near future. In view of this, a programme was started in 1991 to conserve the orchid species of Singapore and the region.

The aim is to increase the species population through seedling culture. Species are being selfed (through artificial self-pollination) or sibbed (artificially pollinated between sibling plants). The resulting seeds are then germinated *in vitro* and seedlings grown to maturity. Once a large population of seedlings is formed and established in the nursery, they can be introduced back to their natural habitats. Since the beginning of the programme, the Gardens has germinated seeds of many species, several of which are growing in the nursery.

In the appendix that follows, a selection of the Gardens' beautiful species are introduced. Many of these species have been used for breeding, and wherever possible, examples of hybrids resulting from these species are mentioned.

The new Cold House for the cool growing orchids

Species of Singapore

Some 180 orchid species representing 58 genera have been recorded in the 633 sq km island of Singapore. Such diversity is due to the existence of a wide range of habitats and the favorable equatorial climate. There arc some unusual species among the Singapore species; examples are *Grammatophyllum speciosum*, the largest orchid plant in the world, and *Taeniophyllum obtusum*, a "leafless" orchid. Here, twenty interesting species in our collection are illustrated.

Bulbophyllum medusae (Lindl.) **Rchb.f.** A native of Singapore, the flowers of this exotic-looking species are creamy yellow, some varieties having purple spots on the floral parts. About 15 of them are arranged in a fan-shaped whorl or in a circle at the tip of the flower stalk. The lateral sepals are 12 cm long, which is much longer than the upper sepal. When the flowers are seen from afar, the lateral sepals look like silk threads hanging on the tree.

Distribution: Thailand, Peninsular Malaysia, Indonesia, Singapore and the Pacific Islands.

Species of Singapore

***Anoectochilus albolineatus* Par. & Rchb.f.** Species belonging to the genus *Anoectochilus* have very interesting, showy leaves, most of them with a network of fine veins. Some species have foliage which appears iridescent in sunlight. Hence, they are known as "jewel orchids". One of the most beautiful is *Anoectochilus albolineatus*. Besides the showy leaves, the species has very extraordinary flowers. The hairy, redbrown sepals and petals are accentuated by a spectacular lip, fringed with 9 filaments that are up to 1 cm long.

Distribution: Indochina, Peninsular Malaysia and Singapore.

***Arachnis hookeriana* (Rchb.f.) Rchb.f.** A typical *Arachnis,* this species has scorpion-shaped flowers, each 5.5 cm across. The sepals and petals are cream-coloured. The lip of the common variety has a purplish mid-lobe, but the variety *luteola* has a pale yellowish green lip. Parent of many arandas and mokaras, the variety *luteola* produces hybrids that are very free-flowering; two examples are *Arachnis* Maggie Oei (*Arachnis hookeriana* var. *luteola* x *Arachnis flosaeris* var. *gracilis*) and *Aranda* Noorah Alsagoff (*Arachnis hookeriana* x *Vanda* Dawn Nishimura).

Distribution: Indochina, Peninsular Malaysia, Borneo and Singapore.

***Arundina graminifolia* (D. Don) Hochr.**
One of the most widespread in Southeast Asia, this species can be found in open grassland, from the lowlands to mountains of several thousand feet. It is also known as the "bamboo orchid" because of its slender bamboo-like leaves. The size of the flower varies considerably, ranging from 4 cm to 8 cm wide. Its petals and sepals are white, flushed with purple towards the tips. The prominent purplish red lip resembles that of *Cattleya*.

Distribution: India, Indochina, China, Thailand, Peninsular Malaysia, Borneo, Indonesia, the Philippines and the Pacific Islands.

***Bulbophyllum vaginatum* (Lindl.) Rchb.f.** A common native orchid of Singapore, *Bulbophyllum vaginatum* is often seen growing on the branches of Rain Trees and *Eugenia grandis*. They usually cover an extensive area of a branch and present a spectacular sight during full bloom. The flowers are creamy yellow. About 15 of them are arranged in a fan-shaped whorl or in a circle at the tip of the scape. The lateral sepals are 7 cm long, which is many times longer than the upper sepal.

Distribution: Thailand, Peninsular Malaysia, Singapore, Borneo and Indonesia.

***Coelogyne mayeriana* Rchb.f.** The flower of this species is characterised by its attractive, clear apple-green petals and sepals. The lip is conspicuously marked with dark red-brown, almost black venations. Because the dark red-brown markings are so intense in some cultivars, the name "Black Orchid" has been given to them. Flowers of two closely related species, *C. pandurata* and *C. asperata*, are very similar to *C. mayeriana*. Unfortunately, the flowers of this beautiful species only last a few days.

Distribution: Thailand, Peninsular Malaysia, Singapore, Borneo and Indonesia.

***Corymborkis veratrifolia* (Reinw.) Bl.** This is a lovely pantropical terrestrial species which is also a native of Singapore. Stems of the plant range from a height of 50 cm to 3 m with leaves 45 cm long by 15 cm across. The 10 to 15-cm-long, branching inflorescences bear numerous, compactly arranged flowers 2 to 3 cm across. The sepals and petals are long and narrow, the former in light green and the latter in white. They are matched by a pointed, graceful white lip. The species grows well under semi-shade.

Distribution: India, Indochina, Myanmar, Thailand, Peninsular Malaysia, Singapore, Borneo, Indonesia, the Philippines, Papua New Guinea and the Pacific Islands.

***Dendrobium crumenatum* Sw.** This is the most common epiphyte in the region frequently seen on roadside trees in Singapore. The species flowers nine days after a heavy rain storm. It is a delight to see them in bloom as the flowers, which resemble white pigeons, are sweetly scented. Unfortunately, the flowers open only for one day.

Distribution: India, Indochina, Myanmar, China, Thailand, Peninsular Malaysia, Borneo, Indonesia, the Philippines and the Pacific Islands.

***Dendrobium leonis* (Lindl.) Rchb.f.** Leaves of this interesting species are thick, fleshy and laterally flattened. Each yellowish green flower is borne near the apex of the stems. The flowers are 1.5 cm across and have an extremely sweet vanilla fragrance which can be detected from a distance. Two hybrids have been produced by this species, one of which is *Dendrobium* Wunderbar's Aporum (*Dendrobium leonis* x *Dendrobium grande*).

Distribution: Indochina, China, Peninsular Malaysia, Singapore, Indonesia and Borneo.

Dendrobium secundum **(Bl.) Lindl.** This exotic-looking species belongs to the section Pedilonum of the genus *Dendrobium*. The leafless stem bears numerous-flowered inflorescences, typical of all species belonging to the section. Several varieties exist, with colours ranging from white and pink to purplish red. The inflorescences are arranged along one side of the pseudobulb. This resembles a bottle brush; hence the common name "bottle brush orchid".

Distribution: Indochina, Myanmar, Thailand, Peninsular Malaysia, Singapore, Borneo, Indonesia and the Philippines.

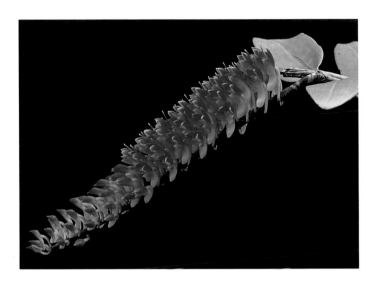

Eria hyacinthoides **(Bl.) Lindl.** As its name indicates, inflorescences of this lovely species emerge near the top of the conical pseudobulbs which resemble those of the hyacinth. Each inflorescence is 15 to 30 cm long and bears 15 to 40 flowers. The sparkling white flowers have a very pleasant translucent appearance.

Distribution: Peninsular Malaysia, Singapore and Indonesia.

***Eria javanica* (Sw.) Bl.** Plants of this inconspicuous species grow in large clumps. A healthy plant can bear inflorescences as long as 40 cm, each with more than 40 flowers. The creamy white flowers are 4 cm across and have a light fragrance. Unfortunately, they are short-lived.

Distribution: India, Myanmar, Indochina, Thailand, Peninsular Malaysia, Singapore, Borneo, Indonesia, the Philippines and Papua New Guinea.

***Eulophia spectabilis* (Dennst.) Suresh.** This terrestrial orchid has 1-m-long inflorescences, each bearing up to 15 flowers. The flower has a rather unique combination of colours. Brownish olive sepals are offset by white petals, and the pale mauve lip has a white patch in the centre.

Distribution: India, Myanmar, Indochina, China, Thailand, Peninsular Malaysia, Singapore, Borneo, Indonesia, the Philippines, Papua New Guinea and the Solomon Islands.

Grammatophyllum speciosum Bl. The name *Grammatophyllum* was derived from two Greek words, *gramma* (letter) and *phyllon* (leaf). It refers to the script-like markings on the sepals and petals of the flowers. This species is also known as the "tiger orchid" because of the markings on the flowers which resemble the skin of a tiger. A mature plant weighs over one ton, making it the largest orchid plant in the world. More than 30 flowers can be borne on the 2-m-long inflorescence. Individual flowers are 10 cm across.

Distribution: Indochina, Peninsular Malaysia, Thailand, Borneo, Indonesia, the Philippines and the Pacific Islands.

***Nephelaphyllum pulchrum* Bl.** The name of the genus is derived from two Greek words, *nephele* (cloud) and *phyllon* (leaf). It refers to the hazy, cloud-like appearance on the upper surface of the leaves. This lovely species has very interesting leaves and delicate flowers. The plant has fleshy, creeping rhizomes. The flowers crowd together on the apical half of the short spike. Because the flowers do not resupinate, the lip points skyward.

Distribution: The Himalayas, India, Myanmar, Indochina, South China, Thailand, Peninsular Malaysia, Singapore, Borneo, Indonesia and the Philippines.

***Phaius tankervilleae* (Banks ex l'Heritier) Bl.** Also known as the "nun orchid", this handsome species has a 1-m-long inflorescence bearing 10 to 20 flowers. Each flower measures up to 12 cm across. The reddish brown petals and sepals are accompanied by a lip ranging from pink to red. Hybrids can be created by crossing *Phaius* with *Calanthe*. An example is *Phaiocalanthe* Centuari (*Phaius tankervilleae* x *Calanthe vestita*).

Distribution: India, China, Indochina, Thailand, Peninsular Malaysia and the Pacific Islands.

Plocoglottis javanica Bl. This inconspicuous plant has long pseudobulbs which bear only one leaf measuring 35 cm long and 10 to 12 cm across. The 80-cm-long flower spike carries some 20 to 30 flowers. Individual flowers measure 1.8 cm across. All floral parts are yellow with red spots. When the flowers first open, the lip points downwards. However, once an insect touches it, the lip springs up towards the column. Such a mechanism is believed to facilitate insect pollination.

Distribution: Thailand, Singapore, Peninsular Malaysia, Borneo and Indonesia.

Spathoglottis plicata Bl. The most common terrestrial orchid of Singapore, the species has an inflorescence that can reach 1.5 to 2 m in length bearing 20 to 30 flowers. There are two varieties of the local species, the dark pink and the alba form. The first hybrid produced by Holttum in the Singapore Botanic Gardens, *Spathoglottis* Primrose, was the progeny of a cross between *Spathoglottis plicata* and *Spathoglottis aurea*. Recently, the Gardens has flowered some new *Spathoglottis* hybrids, one of them a beautiful hybrid which is a cross between *Spathoglottis plicata* var. *alba* and *Spathoglottis kimbaliana*.

Distribution: India, Myanmar, Indochina, Thailand, the Philippines, Papua New Guinea and the Pacific Islands.

Taeniophyllum obtusum **Bl.** A member of a genus also known as "leafless orchids", this species has a greatly reduced stem covered by scale-like leaves. The fleshy green roots which replace the leaves as the photosynthetic organ spread over the bark of its host tree. As the plant is almost flat and its colour blends with its host, one can hardly spot them in their natural habitat. Roots of the plant are about 2 to 3 mm wide. Each flower is 5 mm across. Its petals and sepals are orange-yellow, and the white lip is fleshy and concave. With flowers resembling the figure of a ghost, it is also known as the "ghost orchid".

Distribution: Indochina, Thailand, Peninsular Malaysia, Singapore, Borneo and Indonesia.

Thrixspermum amplexicaule **(Bl.) Rchb.f.** This wide-spread species is one of the semi-aquatic orchids whose lower half is submerged in water. The flowers are very attractive, pale lilac and about 3 cm across. Unfortunately, they last for only a day.

Distribution: The Philippines, Indochina, Thailand, Peninsular Malaysia, Borneo, Indonesia, Papua New Guinea and the Pacific Islands.

Species of Asia Pacific

***Aerides lawrenceae* Rchb.f.** The inflorescence of this beautiful species can reach a length of 45 cm with over 100 compactly arranged, fleshy flowers. Each flower is 3.6 cm across. The petals and sepals are white and blotched dark purple at the tips. The lateral-lobes of the lip are white and the mid-lobe is dark purple. The characteristic spur is greenish with a brown tip. The graceful species gives out a delightful fragrance. This is the most frequently used *Aerides* species for hybridisation.

Distribution: The Philippines.

Some of the most beautiful and extraordinary orchids can be found in the Asia Pacific region. Thousands of orchid species thrive in the numerous habitats ranging from the jungles of tropical Papua New Guinea and Malaya to the subtropical forests in southern China to temperate regions in north Asia. The region is home to some of the most widely cultivated genera, such as *Cymbidium*, *Dendrobium*, *Paphiopedilum* and *Vanda*. The majority of the species in our collection come from the Asia Pacific region.

Species of the Asia Pacific

***Aerides houlletiana* Rchb.f.** This is known to be one of the most superior *Aerides* species. The yellow, orange or brown sepals and petals of the flower are accompanied by a broad and showy lip. The pleasant fragrance imparts special charm to the species. A plant in full bloom is something not to be missed.

Distribution: Indochina.

***Aerides quinquevulnera* Lindl.** An epiphyte from the Philippines, each inflorescence of this species bears numerous dainty fleshy flowers. Each fragrant flower is about 3 cm across. The sepals and petals are white with purple spots and are accompanied by a white lip which has a median band. The spur, which curves forward, is yellow green. Owing to its small flowers, this beautiful species has not been a popular choice for breeding.

Distribution: The Philippines.

Arachnis flosaeris **(L.) Rchb.f.** Flowers belonging to the genus *Arachnis* are scorpion-shaped; hence, they are also known as the scorpion orchids. There are two varieties of the species, *gracilis* and *insignis*. The light green flower of *Arachnis flosaeris* var. *gracilis* is heavily barred with maroon and it releases a musky fragrance. On the other hand, *Arachnis flosaeris* var. *insignis* is known as the "black scorpion orchid". The striking petals and sepals are shiny maroon, almost black in colour; they are contrasted by a white column. Both varieties have very similar vegetative structures. The inflorescence is 5 to 6 feet long and is sometimes branching. Each flower is about 6 cm across. The plant flowers only once or twice a year. *Arachnis flosaeris* var. *gracilis* was one of the parents of *Arachnis* Maggie Oei, an early orchid cut flower of Singapore. Unlike the variety *gracilis*, *Arachnis flosaeris* var. *insignis* is less frequently used for hybridisation because most of its progeny are shy bloomers.

Distribution: Peninsular Malaysia, Borneo, Indonesia and the Philippines.

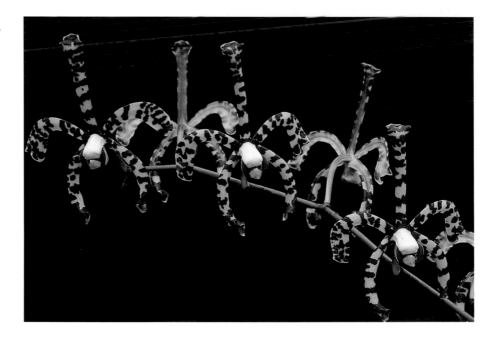

Top: *Arachnis flosaeris* var. *insignis*
Bottom: *Arachnis flosaeris* var. *gracilis*

Bulbophyllum blepharistes **Rchb.f.**
This is one of the few bulbophyllums which has two leaves on the pseudobulb. The inflorescence bears many flowers, of which a few are open at a time. Each flower measures 1.5 cm across. All sepals are light greenish yellow with purple venations and the tiny petals are yellow with a flush of purple and five purple veins. The lateral sepals are fused sideways. The lip is yellow with a purple tint and is spotted in red-purple.

Distribution: Indochina, Thailand and Peninsular Malaysia.

Bulbophyllum gusdorfii **J. J. Sm.** The 6 to 8 flowers of this interesting species are closely arranged in a whorl on a pinkish scape, forming a circlet. The dorsal sepals and petals are fringed with purple hairs. The lateral sepals, which are much longer than the dorsal sepal, are twisted near the base so that their upper edges fuse. Each flower is about 2.5 cm long and 7 to 8 mm across. The pale yellow lateral sepals are flushed with purple near the base. The tiny dorsal sepal is purplish brown while the tongue-shaped lip is purplish green.

Distribution: Thailand, Peninsular Malaysia, Indonesia and the Philippines.

***Bulbophyllum lobbii* Lindl.** This is truly a magnificent species of the region. Individual flowers measure 6 to 10 cm across and are very variable in colour. The sepals of the most common variety are yellow with red stripes. The pseudobulbs are arranged 3 to 8 cm apart, each of which bears a single leaf 10 to 25 cm in length.

Distribution: Myanmar, Indochina, Thailand, Peninsular Malaysia, Indonesia and the Philippines.

***Calanthe vestita* Lindl.** A deciduous species, *Calanthe vestita* blooms around December and January. The 0.5 to 1-m-long erect inflorescence, which is borne on a leafless pseudobulb, bears many white flowers. Each flower is 5 cm across. The characteristic lip has four lobes and a yellow or red callus. *Calanthe vestita* is one of the most widely cultivated and hybridised species of the genus.

Distribution: Myanmar, Indochina, Thailand, Peninsular Malaysia, Borneo, Indonesia and the Philippines.

Cleisomeria lanatum **(Lindl.) ex G. Don.** An unusual-looking species from the region, the plant has a short stem and 10-cm-long, leathery leaves. The flowers cluster together on the branching inflorescences. The petals and sepals are brownish with a green-yellow border, and the fleshy lip is white with purple spots. The surface of the flowers is hairy.

Distribution: Myanmar, Indochina, Thailand and Peninsular Malaysia.

Coelogyne asperata **Lindl.** This handsome species has arching sprays of up to 30 cm in length. Each inflorescence bears many fully opened, well-arranged flowers. The fragrant flowers are 7 cm across. The petals and sepals are light lemon-yellow to cream; the lip has three lobes, the side lobes veined in brown, and the mid-lobe curved downward with two keels and a callus. The species flowers well in Singapore.

Distribution: Peninsular Malaysia, Indonesia, the Philippines, Papua New Guinea and the Pacific Islands.

Cymbidium ensifolium (L.) Sw. Cultivated for thousands of years in China and known as "lan fa", this species is often featured in oriental paintings and pottery. The fragrant flowers vary from greenish white to greenish yellow with brown stripes. The erect inflorescence is 15 cm long, carrying 4 to 7 flowers which measure 5 cm across. For "lan fa" growers, the shape and colour of the leaves are often more important than the flowers.

Distribution: India, Indochina, Peninsular Malaysia, Borneo, China, Japan, the Philippines, Taiwan and Papua New Guinea.

Coelogyne zurowetzii **Carr.** A climber in its natural habitat, this plant has pseudobulbs which adhere closely to the trunk of the host tree. Individual flowers on the inflorescence measure 7 to 8 cm across. The petals and sepals are bright apple green and are accompanied by a warty, light green lip with intense chestnut-brown markings which resemble the body of certain insects. The species flowers regularly under tropical lowland conditions. It was discovered by Carr in the 1930s.

Distribution: Borneo.

***Dendrobium anosmum* Lindl.** Flowers of this widely distributed epiphyte are borne on the leafless stem of the deciduous plant. Each flower measures 8 to 10 cm across. The petals and sepals are pink to orchid purple and are complemented by the broad lip which has a dark purple throat. The flowers have a very nice fragrance but are short-lived.

Distribution: India, Peninsular Malaysia, the Archipelago, Indochina, Indonesia, the Philippines and Papua New Guinea.

***Dendrobium chrysotoxum* Lindl.** This lovely species carries inflorescences of 15 to 20 cm in length, with 10 to 20 gracefully displayed golden-yellow flowers. The flowers have excellent texture and each measures 4 to 5 cm across. The variety *suavissimum* illustrated here has a crimson blotch on the lip throat. In Singapore, the plant flowers occasionally and the flowers last about a week. It would be interesting to introduce the bright golden-yellow colour of this species into the cut-flower dendrobiums by hybridisation.

Distribution: India, Myanmar, Indochina, China and Thailand.

Dendrobium cretaceum Lindl. Several single-flowered inflorescences of this interesting species are borne on both leaf-bearing and leafless pseudobulbs. Each flower measures 3.5 cm across, and all parts are white except for the fine purple veins on the lip.

Distribution: India, Myanmar, Indochina and China.

Dendrobium dearei Rchb.f. A graceful species from the Philippines, the inflorescences are borne towards the apical part of the leafy stem. Each flower measures 5.5 to 6.5 cm across and is pure white except for a light green lip throat. The lasting flowers stay on the plant for several weeks. The species also imparts this long-lasting character to its hybrids. For example, the flowers of *Dendrobium* Singa Dear Mary (*Dendrobium* Mary Trowse x *Dendrobium dearei*) can last for 2 months.

Distribution: The Philippines.

***Dendrobium farmeri* Paxt.** This handsome species displays pendulous inflorescences which bear as many as 30 flowers. The white sepals and petals are matched by a lip with an orange-yellow throat. Unfortunately, the flowers last only several days. This species has been used for hybridisation. An example of this is *Dendrobium* Quek Kiah Huat (*Dendrobium* Udomsri Beauty x *Dendrobium farmeri*), named after a former president of the Orchid Society of South East Asia.

Distribution: India, Indochina, Myanmar, Thailand and Peninsular Malaysia.

***Dendrobium findlayanum* Parish & Rchb.f.** Characterised by the pseudobulbs which swell above the nodes, this lovely species flowers once a year around March and April in Singapore. Each inflorescence carries one to two flowers which measure 6 to 7 cm across. The petals and sepals are light lilac and gradually become white towards the base; the lip is white except for a yellowish-green blotch at the centre.

Distribution: Myanmar, Indochina and Thailand.

Dendrobium formosum Roxb. ex Lindl. A popular showy species, the short inflorescence generally bears 6 to 10 flowers. Each flower measures 7 cm across. The flowers are pure white except for the lip which is a canary yellow in the middle. Two hybrids which have this species in their background are _Dendrobium_ John Nauen (_Dendrobium formosum_ x _Dendrobium ovipositoriferum_) and _Dendrobium_ Dawn Maree (_Dendrobium formosum_ x _Dendrobium cruentum_).

Distribution: Northern India, Himalayan region, Myanmar, Indochina and Thailand.

Dendrobium helix Cribb This interesting species is a member of the section _Spatulata_. Species in this section have two curly petals which resemble the horns of an antelope; hence, they are also known as the "antelope orchids". The erect inflorescences carry 10 to 20 flowers. There are several varieties of the species. The common variety has yellowish green curly petals, whereas the variety 'Pomio Brown' has brown floral parts. This species has been used extensively for breeding. An example of a recent hybrid of the Singapore Botanic Gardens is _Dendrobium_ Yuen-Peng McNeice (_Dendrobium_ Tan Nam Keow x _Dendrobium helix_), named after the wife of Sir Percy McNeice.

Distribution: New Britain.

***Dendrobium lasianthera* J. J. Sm.** In spite of its enormous pseudobulbs, this species dwells on trees in its native habitat. This beautiful antelope *Dendrobium* produces erect inflorescences that last several months. The petals are glossy dark maroon with yellow borders, and the sepals are white without coloured borders. Of all the varieties, 'Sepik Blue' and 'May River Red' are the most beautiful. Several hybrids of the Singapore Botanic Gardens having this species as a parent are *Dendrobium* Joseph Chew, *Dendrobium* Tan Chye Siam, and *Dendrobium* Margaret Thatcher.

Distribution: Papua New Guinea.

***Dendrobium lineale* Rolfe** A mature plant of this giant antelope orchid can bear numerous 50 to 70-cm-long inflorescences, displaying more than 30 well-spaced flowers on each. There are many varieties of the species. The flowers of the most popular one are white except for the lip which is veined with purple. Being free-flowering and vigorous, many of today's cut-flower hybrids have this species in their background.

Distribution: Papua New Guinea, the Solomon Islands and Bougainville.

Dendrobium moschatum **(Buch.-Ham.)
Sw.** This attractive species bears flowers 7 to 8 cm across and in pleasing colours. The petals and sepals are peach-coloured with some lilac veins, and the lip is an unusual pouch shape, with two dark purple blotches on its throat. Unfortunately, the delightful musk-scented flowers last only a few days.

Distribution: India, Myanmar, Indochina and Thailand.

Dendrobium nindii **W. Hill** An antelope *Dendrobium*, this well-grown plant displays several upright sprays with numerous flowers. The sepals and petals are white except for a flush of lilac on the latter. The large and attractive lip is delicately veined in purple. It has been used extensively for breeding, an example of which is *Dendrobium* Premier Yusof (*Dendrobium nindii* x *Dendrobium* Anita).

Distribution: Australia and Papua New Guinea.

***Dendrobium smillieae* F. Muell.** The inflorescence of this member of the section *Pedilonum* bears numerous flowers and is borne towards the apical part of the leafless stem. Each flower is 1.5 to 2 cm long. All floral parts are white to pale green with darker green tips. The fleshy flowers are very lasting.

Distribution: Papua New Guinea and Australia.

Dendrobium spectabile (Bl.) Miq. This is one of the more curious-looking species from Papua New Guinea. Each fleshy flower measures 7 to 8 cm across. The sepals and petals are light yellow-green with intense dull purple venations. The lip is heavily spotted with dark brown. The margins of all the floral parts are wavy. Flowers of this spectacular species are very lasting. Many hybrids have been created using this plant, one example being *Dendrobium* Violet Yamaji (*Dendrobium* Midnight x *Dendrobium spectabile*).

Distribution: Papua New Guinea and the Pacific Islands.

Dendrobium stratiotes Rchb.f. Another member of the section *Spatulata*, this species has flowers arranged symmetrically on its sub-erect inflorescence. The creamy-white sepals are contrasted by two light green, erect petals. The pointed lip is white with pronounced purple veins. The good-textured flowers are lasting; hence, it has been used frequently for hybridisation.

Distribution: Papua New Guinea and the Solomon Islands.

***Dendrobium tangerinum* Cribb.** An attractive species, *Dendrobium tangerinum* has many unique characteristics of its own. A flowering plant bears several flower spikes, each carrying 5 to 15 flowers. Each flower measures 3 cm across. The sepals and petals are an unusual brown-orange to orange-red. The narrow mid-lobe of the lip, which bends downwards, has three lilac keels. This species has been used to create several hybrids in our breeding programme, an example of which is *Dendrobium* Richard Hale (*Dendrobium* Garnet Beauty x *Dendrobium tangerinum*).

Distribution: Papua New Guinea.

***Dendrobium taurinum* Lindl.** This lovely Philippine species bears inflorescences of 20 to 50 cm in length, with some 20 flowers. The sepals are light cream with a tinge of green, which contrast beautifully with the purple petals and the showy lip. The most outstanding feature of this species is the large and brightly coloured lip which is transmitted to most of its offspring. Several outstanding hybrids of the Singapore Botanic Gardens were made using *Dendrobium taurinum*; they are *Dendrobium* Elina Jayewardene, *Dendrobium* Lady Dibela, *Dendrobium* Lady Hochoy and *Dendrobium* Temasek.

Distribution: The Philippines.

***Doritis pulcherrima* Lindl.** The erect inflorescences of this showy species are branched and can measure up to 45 cm, often bearing more than 20 flowers. Individual flowers measure 2.5 to 3 cm across. There are many varieties of this species, the flowers ranging from pure white to dark rosy purple.

The variety *buysonniana* is a tetraploid. The species is interfertile with *Phalaenopsis* and some other vandaceous species.

Distribution: Indochina, China, Myanmar, Thailand, Peninsular Malaysia, Borneo and Indonesia.

***Eria multiflora* (Bl.) Lindl.**
Plants of this splendid species bear numerous inflorescences during the blooming season. Each 30 to 35-cm-long pseudobulb can bear up to 5 inflorescences. Each of them can display over 100 small flowers. The flowers are 5 to 6 mm across, white to light pink, except for a violet flush on the lip. Unfortunately, the plant does not flower frequently.

Distribution: Java, Sumatra and Bali.

***Eria pubescens* (Hook.) Steud.**
Pseudobulbs of this interesting species are distinctly flattened, each bearing 4 leaves. This unusual-looking species is characterised by the woolly inflorescence which bears several flowers. The lasting flowers open a few at a time. The petals and sepals are green and covered by fine hairs on the external surface. A grey-purple lip provides the contrast. This species is variable and widely distributed.

Distribution: The Himalayas, Indochina, China, Peninsular Malaysia and Indonesia.

Eria xanthocheila Ridl. The 8 to 10-cm-long inflorescences of this attractive species emerge from the top of the 25 to 30-cm-long pseudobulbs. Each bears some 15 dainty flowers with individuals measuring 1.5 cm across. The sepals and petals are pale yellow and are complemented by a darker yellow lip. The flowers last only a few days.

Distribution: Myanmar Peninsular Malaysia, Borneo and Indonesia.

Euanthe sanderiana (Rchb.f.) Schltr. This native of the Philippines is one of the most well-known species in the orchid world. The attractive flowers are round, with overlapping floral parts. The diameter of some outstanding cultivars can reach 11 to 12 cm. The dorsal sepals and petals are light pink with some brown spots; the lateral sepals are heavily spotted with brown. *Euanthe sanderiana* has been used extensively for breeding.

Distribution: The Philippines.

***Eulophia andamanensis* Rchb.f.** *Eulophia* is a pantropical genus with more than 200 species. Most of them are found in Africa. Inflorescences of this common terrestrial are borne on the 10-cm-tall, leafless pseudobulbs. Each inflorescence displays 10 to 15 flowers. The individual flower measures 2.5 cm across and is green except for the lip which is marked with brown veins.

Distribution: Burma, Indochina, Thailand, Peninsular Malaysia, Indonesia and Taiwan.

***Flickingeria comata* (Bl.) Hawkes** Flowers of this peculiar-looking species are borne on the internodes of the pseudobulbs. The petals and sepals are creamy yellow with purple spots. The most interesting part of the flower is the deep irregularly clefted lip. Its flowers last only one day. *Dendrogeria* Mistique (*Dendrobium* Ellen x *Flickingeria comata*) is an interesting hybrid of this species.

Distribution: Thailand, Peninsular Malaysia, Borneo, Indonesia, Papua New Guinea, N. E. Australia, the Pacific Islands and Taiwan.

***Geesinkorchis alaticallosa* de Vogel** This free-flowering species bears inflorescences of over 50 cm long with some 70 flowers which open successively. Each flower measures 1.2 cm across. The sepals and petals are yellow-brown. The lip is yellow-brown with a brown blotch in the centre. On top of the column is its characteristic hood. The genus was named after Dr. R. Geesink of Leiden's Rijksherbarium in the Netherlands.

Distribution: Borneo.

***Geodorum citrinum* Jacks.** This uncommon terrestrial orchid has interesting inflorescences which droop like a shepherd's stick. The yellow flowers are 3 to 4 cm across. The unusual-looking, pail-like lip is lightly veined in red.

Distribution: India, Myanmar, Thailand and Peninsular Malaysia.

***Habenaria rhodocheila* Hance**. There is no doubt that this is one of the most colourful terrestrial species found in this region. The plant bears 6 leaves, and the terminal inflorescence carries some 10 flowers. Individual flowers are 2 cm across. The petals and sepals are green, and the showy lip ranges from bright yellow to pink and orange. The best varieties of the species have been crossed to produce some of the most spectacular potted plants.

Distribution: South China, Indochina, Thailand and Peninsular Malaysia.

***Liparis maingayi* (Hook.f.) Ridl.** The oval-shaped fleshy leaves of this unusual-looking species measure 10 to 14 cm long and 5 to 10 cm across. The deep purple flowers are borne on a 10 to 15-cm-long inflorescence, and they measure 1 cm long and 6 mm across. The petals and sepals are slender while the 5-mm-long lip is divided into two halves, each with 3 to 4 teeth. The plant thrives better and flowers well inside the Cold House.

Distribution: Thailand, Peninsular Malaysia and Indonesia.

Paphiopedilum barbatum **(Lindl.) Pfitz.**
Species belonging to the genus *Paphiopedilum*
are also known as "Lady Slipper Orchids" because of the pouch-like lip which resembles a
lady's slipper. The leaves of this terrestrial orchid are 10 to 20 cm long and 2 to 3 cm broad,
with some dark green patches. The inflorescence bears a single flower measuring some 8
cm across. The dorsal sepal is white with some
purple stripes and a flush of green; the petals
are purple with darker brown-purple stripes,
with some black hairy warts at the upper
edges; the lip is a complementary brown-purple that becomes paler towards its base. Although the plant can flower outdoors in Singapore, it grows much better in the Cold House.

Distribution: Peninsular Malaysia and
Penang.

Paphiopedilum lowii **(Lindl.) Stein**. A mature plant of this beautiful semi-epiphytic orchid can reach a height of up to 1 m, with
leaves measuring 30 cm long and 4 cm wide.
The 50 to 100-cm-long inflorescences bear 2 to
4 showy flowers. Individual blooms are 10 to
14 cm wide. The dorsal sepal is light yellow-
green with purple-brown lines which intensify
towards the centre. The drooping petals are
very colourful, light yellow-green with purple-
brown blotches; they dramatically contrast
with a purple apex. The green pouch-shaped
lip is heavily suffused with brown markings.
Since the species is found only at 1,000 to
1,600 m above sea level, it can only flower in
the Cold House.

Distribution: Peninsular Malaysia, Borneo
and Indonesia.

***Papilionanthe hookeriana* (Rchb.f.) Schltr.** More commonly known as *Vanda hookeriana*, the species is one of the parents of *Vanda* Miss Joaquim, the national flower of Singapore. Because it inhabits the swampy country in Johore and in the Kinta Valley of Perak, it is also known as the "Kinta Weed". There are two varieties of the species: the common one has light mauve petals and a dorsal sepal, with a broad prominent lip which is spotted with purple; the other is a pure white variety which has been used extensively for breeding white hybrids. Examples are *Vanda* Poepoe 'Diana' and *Vanda* Miss Joaquim 'John Laycock'.

Distribution: Indochina, Thailand, Peninsular Malaysia, Borneo and Indonesia.

***Papilionanthe teres* (Roxb.) Schltr.** Also known as *Vanda teres*, it is the other parent of *Vanda* Miss Joaquim (*Vanda teres* x *Vanda hookeriana*). There are several varieties of the species. Two of the more common varieties are *aurorea* and *andersoni*. The former has purplish petals, whereas the latter has a characteristic orange-yellow throat. The other two lesser known varieties are *gigantea* and the alba variety *candida*. This lovely species has been used extensively for hybridisation, one of its well known progeny being *Vanda* Emma van Deventer.

Distribution: India, the Himalayas, Myanmar, South China, Indochina and Thailand.

Vanda Miss Joaquim 'Agnes'

Vanda Miss Joaquim 'Josephine'

Right: *Vanda* Miss Joaquim 'Douglas'

***Paraphalaenopsis denevei* J.J. Sm.** This is one of the four species of the genus *Paraphalaenopsis*. They are also known as the "Rat Tail" *Phalaenopsis* as its terete leaves resemble the tails of rats! The short inflorescence bears 4 to 15 flowers of good substance, measuring 5 to 6 cm across. The sepals and petals are golden brown; all three lobes of the lip are crimson and the lip throat is white with crimson spots. This lovely species has been used for producing many outstanding hybrids, one of them being *Vandaenopsis* Khoo Kay Ann (*Paraphalaenopsis denevei* x *Vanda* Prolific).

Distribution: Borneo.

***Paraphalaenopsis labukensis* Lam, Chan & Shim** The most noticeable feature of this rat tail orchid is its 2-m-long leaves. Some 10 to 20 flowers are borne on the short inflorescence. The flowers are of good texture and are 5 to 6 cm across. The sepals and petals are dark golden brown surrounded by a yellow margin. Only a few hybrids have been made since its recent discovery, an example of which is *Paraphalaenopsis* Kimmy (*Paraphalaenopsis labukensis* x *Paraphalaenopsis denevei*).

Distribution: Borneo.

Phalaenopsis amabilis **(L.) Bl.** This is one of the most beautiful and well-known species around. The 40 to 100-cm-long inflorescences hang down gracefully from the short stem. Each spray bears many well-arranged, round flowers. They vary from 5 to 10 cm in diameter. The showy flowers are lightly scented and are long lasting. The magnificent white flowers can last for a few months on the plant. Its long lifespan and the sizeable, well-arranged flowers make it one of the most popular species for hybridisation.

Distribution: Peninsular Malaysia, Borneo, Indonesia, Papua New Guinea and the Philippines.

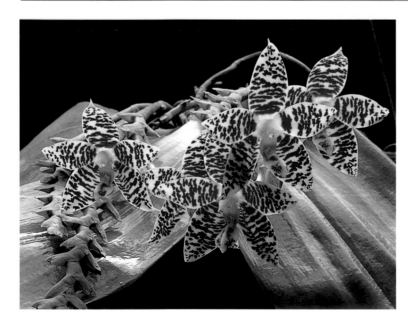

Phalaenopsis amboinensis **J.J. Sm.** Inflorescences of this delightful species bear 3 to 6 star-shaped flowers of good substance. The two colour forms — white and golden-yellow — occur in nature, and both are barred with cinnamon. The species is frequently used for breeding yellow hybrids and is the parent of a well-known local award winning hybrid, *Phalaenopsis* Amber Delight 'Benjamin' AM OSSEA (*Phalaenopsis* Teoh Tee Teong x *Phalaenopsis amboinensis*).

Distribution: Sulawesi and the Moluccas.

***Phalaenopsis lueddemanniana*
Rchb.f.** Borne on the long and branching inflorescences of this species, the star-shaped flowers measure some 6 to 7 cm across. This species is genetically variable with many different varieties. The sepals and petals vary in colour from cream with red bars to yellow or greenish yellow with brown bars. It has been used extensively for creating *Phalaenopsis* hybrids with novelty colours.

Distribution: The Philippines.

***Phalaenopsis schilleriana*
Rchb.f.** The branching inflorescences of the outstanding plant bear more than 200 showy flowers. Each flower measures 7 cm across. The petals and sepals are pink, turning white towards the margins. The lateral-lobes of the lip are light yellow with some heavy brown spots towards the base and the mid-lobe is white with purple spots. The apex has appendages which curve upward. This is an important species used by breeders to produce the multi-flower type of *Phalaenopsis* hybrids.

Distribution: The Philippines.

Phalaenopsis stuartiana Rchb.f.
A charming species from the Philippines, it bears many showy flowers, each of which is 6 to 7 cm in diameter. The floral parts are white, except for the inner sides of the lateral sepals and the lip which are spotted in brown. The lip is distinguished by the two tail-like protrusions on the mid-lobe. This is another species which has been used extensively for breeding.

Distribution: The Philippines.

Phalaenopsis violacea Witte This variable species has two major forms: the Borneo-type and the Peninsular Malaysia-type. The former is more uniform in its shape, size and basic colour; individual flowers are about 4 cm across; the sepals and petals are white except for the inner half of the lateral sepals and lip which are magenta-purple. The Peninsular Malaysia-type is more variable; flowers measure 5 cm across, their colour ranging from pure white to dark rosy purple with green tips. The species is graced with a sweet fragrance.

Distribution: Peninsular Malaysia, Borneo and Indonesia.

***Renanthera bella* J.J. Wood.** A recently discovered *Renanthera* species, its radiant red flowers are borne on a branching inflorescence with individual flowers measuring 4 cm across. The compact plant has been used for hybridisation in the Singapore Botanic Gardens.

Distribution: Borneo.

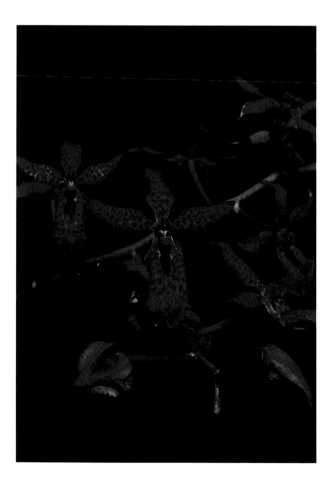

***Renanthera philippinensis* Ames & Quis.** As its name indicates, this fiery species is a native of the Philippines. Each 60 to 80-cm-long inflorescence bears numerous, slightly scented flowers. Each flower is 3.5 cm in diameter and blood-red in colour except for the cream lateral-lobes of the lip and the orange lip throat. Even though its flowers are smaller than *Renanthera storiei*, it is known to impart its compactness and floriferousness to its progeny. *Renanthera* Kalsom, a primary hybrid between *Renanthera philippinensis* and *Renanthera storiei*, has inherited the compactness from the former and the flower size from the latter.

Distribution: The Philippines.

***Rhynchostylis gigantea* (Lindl.) Ridl.** Also known as the "Fox Tail Orchid", flowers of this species are rather variable in colour, ranging from pure white, light pink speckled with purple to deep purple specks. Individual flowers are 2.5 to 3 cm across. Its long lifespan and numerous, well-arranged flowers make it a popular species for hybridisation. An example of its progeny is *Arachnostylis* Chorchalood.

Distribution: Indochina, Myanmar, China, Thailand, Peninsular Malaysia and Borneo.

***Rhynchostylis retusa* (L.) Bl.** This showy species bears drooping inflorescences of 20 to 40 cm in length, with numerous compactly arranged flowers measuring 2 cm across. There are two varieties of the species: the common one has white petals and sepals with purple spots, and the rare alba variety is completely white. The species flowers well in Singapore.

Distribution: Sri Lanka, the northwestern Himalayas, South China, Peninsular Malaysia, the Philippines and Indonesia.

***Spathoglottis affinis* de Vriese** The word *Spathoglottis* comes from two Latin words, *Spathe* (spathe) and *glotta* (tongue), referring to the broad mid-lobe of the lip of the genus. In this deciduous plant, 10 to 20 flowers are spaced out along the slender spike. The colour of the flowers varies from a pale to a deep rich yellow. At the time of writing, the Gardens is still anticipating the outcome of the crosses made between *Spathoglottis affinis* and some of the lowland *Spathoglottis* species. The idea is to combine the spacious flower arrangement form of the former with the free-flowering characteristics of the latter.

Distribution: Myanmar, Indochina, Thailand, Peninsular Malaysia, Borneo and Indonesia.

***Spathoglottis vanoverberghii* Ames.** A native of the Philippines, this terrestrial orchid, with cylindrical pseudobulbs, has short spikes which bear 4 to 6 bright yellow flowers. It is leafless during the blooming season. Individual flowers measure 3.5 cm across. Unlike other *Spathoglottis*, flowers of this species are very lasting; hence it has been used rather regularly in breeding.

Distribution: The Philippines.

Trichoglottis loheriana (**Kränzl.**) **L.O. Wms.** This attractive species has a 20 to 30-cm-long inflorescence which bears 10 to 25 fleshy flowers measuring 2.2 cm across. The oblong sepals and petals are light green and spotted with brown; they are complemented by a fleshy lip with three lobes, the mid-lobe being white with red spots.

Distribution: The Philippines.

Trichoglottis philippinensis **Lindl.** A native of the Philippines, it bears many single-flower inflorescences along the stem. Each flower measures 4.5 cm across. The sepals and petals are ruby red and are characteristically edged with a thin yellow margin. The lip is imperial purple and divided into three lobes with hairs at the centre of the mid-lobe. A small yellow tongue is situated at the back of the lip.

Distribution: The Philippines.

***Vanda dearei* Rchb.f.** The short inflorescence of this species carries 2 to 5 flowers, each 6 to 7 cm in diameter. The lemon-yellow flowers of heavy substance emit a pleasant fragrance in the morning. Most hybrids of *Vanda dearei* are fragrant. Examples are *Aranda* Nancy (*Arachnis hookeriana* x *Vanda dearei*) and *Vanda* Mark Shou Young (*Vanda dearei* x *Vanda luzonica*).

Distribution: Borneo.

***Vanda insignis* Bl.** A native of Java, this Indonesian species bears 10-cm-long inflorescences with 3 to 6 spirally-arranged flowers. The petals and sepals of this colourful species are shiny chestnut brown. The good texture and showy lip of the flowers make *Vanda insignis* a popular candidate for hybridisation. One of its most outstanding progeny is the well-known amphidiploid, *Vanda* Josephine van Brero (*Vanda insignis* x *Vanda teres*). This hybrid has in turn been used to produce numerous peach and yellow-orange plants such as the world renowned *Vanda* Tan Chay Yan (*Vanda dearei* x *Vanda* Josephine van Brero).

Distribution: Java.

Vanda sumatrana Schltr. A robust epiphyte, the species has short inflorescences which bear only a few flowers of good substance. Each 4-cm-wide flower has waxy olive-brown sepals and petals, which gradually change to red-brown towards the base. The lip is light brown, becoming white towards its throat. It has a very strong fragrance, especially in the early morning. One beautiful hybrid which has *Vanda sumatrana* as a parent is *Vanda* Alice Laycock.

Distribution: Sumatra.

Vanda tricolor Lindl. The semi-erect inflorescence of this delightful species displays some 10 well-displayed flowers. The fragrant flowers have good substance and measure about 7 cm in diameter. There are several varieties of the species: the sepals and petals of the variety *suavis* has a white background with a few red-purple spots and a purple lip; the variety *pallida*, however, is white spotted in yellow-green. Many of today's fine hybrids are the progeny of *Vanda tricolor*, an example of which is the famous *Aranda* Hilda Galistan (*Arachnis hookeriana* x *Vanda tricolor* var. *suavis*).

Distribution: Indonesia and the Philippines.

***Vandopsis gigantea* (Lindl.) Pfitz.** As the name indicates, this is a gigantic plant which flowers once a year in Singapore. The leaves of the species reach a length of 35 cm. The inflorescence, which is about 20 to 30 cm long, bears 10 to 15 flowers. The heavy substanced flowers are yellow with brown blotches. It is interfertile with other vandaceous species; however, its bulky vegetative structures render it unpopular for hybridisation.

Distribution: Myanmar, Indochina, China, Thailand and the Langkawi Islands of Malaysia.

***Vandopsis warocqueana* Schltr.** This is yet another giant-sized *Vandopsis* species with 35-cm-long leaves. The flowers are borne on 25 to 35-cm-long, branching inflorescences. Individual flowers are 2.5 cm in diameter, having a dull yellow background with some brown-red spots. This native species has been used for producing only a few hybrids.

Distribution: Papua New Guinea.

Oeceoclades saundersiana
(Rchb.f.) Garay & Taylor A
rather widespread African terrestrial with dark green
pseudobulbs which grow above
ground, the species possesses
very unusual-coloured flowers
of good shape. Individual flowers are 2.5 to 3.5 cm across. All
floral parts are yellow with
dark purplish brown markings.

Distribution: Tropical Africa.

Species of Africa

It is estimated that some
1,500 species of orchids
can be found in the
continent of Africa and
Madagascar. The orchids
of Africa are very different
from the colourful and
showy species of the
Americas and Asia. They
are considered rather
unusual species and are
also known to be more
challenging to grow. Some
of the better known genera
are *Angraecum, Aerangis,
Cyrtorchis, Disa, Ansellia*
and *Bulbophyllum*. All of
the species illustrated
here grow well in the
Gardens.

Species of Africa

***Angraecum eburneum* Bory** The name of the genus is derived from the Malay word *angurek*, which refers to epiphytic orchids. This exotic-looking plant is one of the 200 species of the genus *Angraecum*. Each rigid inflorescence can bear as many as 30 well-arranged waxy flowers. The flowers do not resupinate. Each of them measures up to 10 cm in diameter. The sepals and petals are yellow-green and the heart-shaped lip is concave, with a 6 to 7-cm-long spur.

Distribution: Comoro Islands, Mascarene Islands, Madagascar and East Africa.

Angraecum sesquipedale Thou. The star-shaped flowers of this special species are fleshy and waxy. Each white flower measures 13 to 15 cm across, with a 30 to 35-cm-long spur. Charles Darwin hypothesized that the long spur in the flower would require a moth with an equally long proboscis for pollination. His suggestion was proven to be true when a hawk-moth *Xanthopan morganii praedicta* was discovered to be the pollinator.

Distribution: Madagascar.

Angraecum leonis (Rchb.f.) Veitch. The characteristic leaves of this lovely species are curved and laterally compressed. Each inflorescence bears up to 7 flowers. The ivory-white flowers are fleshy and measure 4 to 5 cm in diameter. The lip is concave and is characterised by a 7 to 9-cm-long spur.

Distribution: Comoro Islands and Madagascar.

Bulbophyllum barbigerum **Lindl.**
This is one of the most peculiar-looking species in the Gardens' collection. The flowers of this interesting native of Africa measure some 2 cm across. The three sepals are yellow-green with a flush of purple. The most interesting feature is the hairy lip which is highly sensitive to the slightest air movement. The species grows and flowers well in Singapore.

Distribution: Sierra Leone, Cameroon and Zaire.

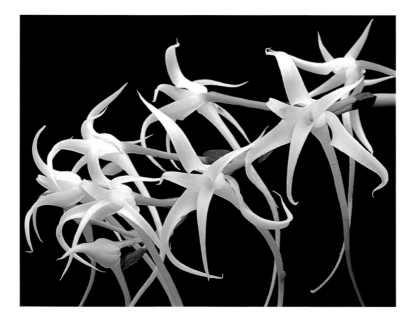

Cyrtorchis arcuata **(Lindl.) Schltr.** This exotic species begins to flower at a very short height and displays several beautiful sprays. The translucent, ivory-white flower is 6 to 8 cm across. The curved petals and sepals are accompanied by a long and slender spur. So far, this beautiful species has only produced one hybrid: *Angraeorchis* Mad (*Angraecum eichlerianum* x *Cyrtorchis arcuata*).

Distribution: Tropical and South Africa.

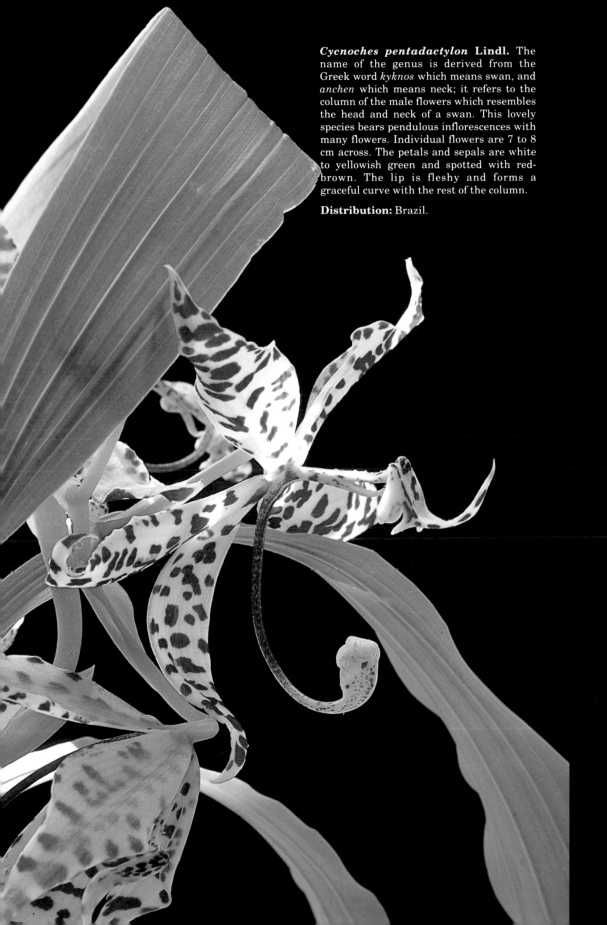

***Cycnoches pentadactylon* Lindl.** The name of the genus is derived from the Greek word *kyknos* which means swan, and *anchen* which means neck; it refers to the column of the male flowers which resembles the head and neck of a swan. This lovely species bears pendulous inflorescences with many flowers. Individual flowers are 7 to 8 cm across. The petals and sepals are white to yellowish green and spotted with red-brown. The lip is fleshy and forms a graceful curve with the rest of the column.

Distribution: Brazil.

Species of the Americas

The Americas is home to many colourful and large-flowered species This includes species belonging to genera such as *Brassavola, Sophronites, Epidendrum, Miltonia* the *Cattleya* alliance, *Oncidium* and its alliance, and numerous other unusual species. The Singapore Botanic Gardens' collection consists of many species of *Oncidium* and representatives from various other genera. Many of them are shown here.

Species of the Americas

Brassavola nodosa (L.) Lindl. This epiphyte of tropical South America has an inflorescence which bears several flowers, each flower measuring 7 to 8 cm across. The slender, pale green petals and sepals are complemented by a broad white lip. *Brassavola nodosa* has been used frequently as a parent for breeding.

Distribution: From Mexico to Colombia on the Pacific coast and throughout the Caribbean Coast and islands.

Catasetum pileatum Rchb.f. The male inflorescence of the most common variety of the species has waxy white flowers with a fleshy, heart-shaped lip. Catasetum's very effective mechanism of pollination is carried out by bees. Two to three days after opening, the male flowers produce a musky smell which attracts the male bees. The bees fly towards the flowers and touch the two long antennae on the column. Extremely sensitive to touch, the antennae trigger the ejection of the pollinia onto the body of the bees. The pollinia, which are stuck securely by the sticky viscidium, are then inserted into the stigma of the female flower.

Distribution: Venezuela, Colombia, Trinidad and Brazil.

Catasetum saccatum
Lindl. This is another unusual species from South America. The pendulous male inflorescence bears many flowers. The sepals and petals have an unusual olive-brown colour with green markings. The heavily fringed mid-lobe of the lip is deep purple brown and the lateral-lobes are green.

Distribution: Peru, Ecuador, Brazil, Guyana and Colombia.

Caularthron bicornutum **(Hook.) R. E. Schultes.** A South American species which adapts well to our local climate, the plant flowers almost throughout the year. The inflorescence bears 10 to 20 flowers, but only a few open at a time. The spectacular white flowers are 6 cm in diameter and are very fragrant. The species can hybridise readily with many species in the Laeliinae sub-tribe. For registration of hybrids, the species still uses its old name *Diacrium bicornutum*.

Distribution: Venezuela, southern Caribbean Islands and Amazonian South America.

Encyclia fragrans **(Sw.) Lemeé.** The inflorescence of this South American species situated on the single-leafed oblong pseudobulb carries several fragrant, non-resupinate flowers. Individual flowers are 5 to 6 cm across, the petals and sepals are pale green, and the white lip is striped with purple veins.

Distribution: Mexico, Central America, northern part of South America and the West Indies.

Gongora quinquenervis Ruiz & Pavón. The peculiar-looking flowers of this South American species hang on the pendulous, 50 to 80-cm-long inflorescence. The flowers are slightly scented. The slender sepals and petals are brown with yellow bands, contrasting with the curious fleshy lip of creamy yellow.

Distribution: Tropical South America from Mexico to Bolivia and Trinidad.

Epidendrum ibaguense **H.B.K.** Stems of this colourful terrestrial can grow up to a metre in height. Each inflorescence carries many closely arranged flowers which are 2 to 3 cm across. The flowers, which vary considerably in colour, range from magenta, scarlet and orange to the rarer alba form. The species has been used for hybridisation, and one of its outstanding hybrids is *Epidendrum* Rung Aroon (*Epidendrum cinnabarinum* x *Epidendrum ibaguense*).

Distribution: Colombia and Venezuela.

***Ionopsis utricularioides* (Sw.) Lindl.** The genus name of this beautiful species means "violet-like", which refers to its flowers. Flowers are borne on the branching inflorescences which can reach a length of 70 cm. Individual flowers are white to light pink with darker pink stripes. The most showy part of the flower is the prominent lip.

The 5-mm-wide sepals and petals are located above the lip. The species has been crossed successfully with other species within the Oncidiinae subtribe.

Distribution: Florida, West Indies, Mexico to Peru, Venezuela, the Guyana and Brazil.

***Oncidium lanceanum* Lindl.** An attractive native of South America, it is a very popular plant for the tropical lowlands. The 30-cm-long inflorescence bears some 12 flowers, each one 6 cm across. Individual flowers are very showy; the sepals and petals have a yellow background which is heavily spotted with purple-brown dots, beautifully contrasted with a violet-purple lip. This species is frequently used for hybridisation. One of its hybrids is *Oncidium* Haematochiulum (*Oncidium lanceanum* x *Oncidium luridum*).

Distribution: From Venezuela to Peru, the Guyana and the West Indies.

***Oncidium sphacelatum* Lindl.** One of the parents of the well-known *Oncidium* Goldiana (*Oncidium flexuosum* x *Oncidium spacelatum*), this species flowers freely in Singapore. The branching inflorescence can reach a length of 2 m, producing numerous flowers. Each flower is about 3 cm in diameter. The sepals and petals are yellow with several broad, chestnut-brown bars across them. They are accompanied by a prominent lip which is bright yellow with a brown bar before the callus.

Distribution: Mexico to El Salvador.

***Peristeria elata* Hook**. The genus *Peristeria* is derived from the Greek word *peristerion* which means dove. It refers to the structures at the centre of the flower which resemble a dove with its out-stretched wings. Hence, the orchid is also known as the "holy ghost orchid" or the "dove orchid". This national flower of Panama has large pseudobulbs about 8 cm in diameter. The leaves are apple green attaining 1 m in length. Each inflorescence can reach a length of 1.3 m, bearing more than 20 scented flowers. The waxy flowers are ivory white with some rose-red spots on the lip.

Distribution: Panama, Costa Rica, Venezuela and Colombia.

***Rhyncholaelia digbyana* (Lindl.) Schltr.** This South American species is characterised by the unusually large lip that is deeply fringed at its border. Individual flowers range from 15 to 20 cm across and are light green. Owing to its large and fragrant flower and its distinctive lip, the species has been used extensively for breeding with cattleyas and other intergeneric hybrids.

Distribution: Mexico and Belize.

***Sophronitis cernua* Lindl.** A native of Bolivia and Brazil, this lovely miniature species produces attractive, brilliant orange flowers with a complementary lighter yellow-orange lip. Individual flowers are 2.5 cm across. When used for breeding, the species imparts the bright orange colour to its hybrids.

Distribution: Bolivia and Brazil.

***Trigonidium egertonianum* Batem. ex Lindl.** Flowers of this unusual-looking species are triangular-shaped and measure about 3 cm in diameter. The most dominant feature of the flower is the sepals which are yellowish green with some olive-brown veins. The inconspicuous petals have a bluish thickening. This peculiar unorchid-like species flowers throughout the year.

Distribution: Mexico to Ecuador.

The author conducts hybridisation at the new Orchid Nursery.
Inset: Pollination is a process by which the pollen from the male parent is inserted into the stigma of the female parent.

Establishing a breeding programme

Since the beginning of the breeding programme in 1928, the Singapore Botanic Gardens has been creating numerous hybrids for landscaping, cut-flower production and potted plants. To meet the specific requirements of each purpose, breeding goals are set.

Under the tropical lowland climate of Singapore, most species of orchids do not flower throughout the year. Inspired by the free-flowering *Vanda* Miss Joaquim, Holttum began a breeding programme to produce free-flowering and colourful hybrids with the aim to brighten up gardens and landscapes. That was an extremely significant breakthrough that has since transformed many public gardens, not only in Singapore but throughout the region, many hybrids from the programme becoming important landscaping materials.

For landscaping plants, the programme concentrates on sun-loving genera such as *Dendrobium, Arachnis, Aranda, Ascocenda, Mokara, Aranthera, Renantanda,* semi and quarter-terete vandas and *Spathoglottis.* The hybrids must meet the following criteria:

- attractive colours — although several decades of breeding have produced numerous colourful hybrids, more new colours can still be created.

- free-flowering — this characteristic is extremely important in order to provide colour to the tropical landscape throughout the year.
- fast growing — the aim is to produce hybrids that can flower within 24 months from the time of planting of seedlings.
- disease-free — in order to reduce maintenance work and the use of chemicals, plants should be resistant to the major diseases.

As the breeding programme developed, researchers soon discovered that many of the orchid hybrids, besides being colourful and free-flowering, lasted for as long as three to four weeks. Hence, they were most suitable for the cut-flower industry. Attempts were then made to create plants whose flowers packed and travelled well, and with the advent of air cargo, cut flower exports to Europe became a promising industry. During the 60s and 70s, hybrids made by the Singapore Botanic Gardens formed the backbone of a lucrative export trade, with farmers relying on the Gardens for their plant materials.

A landscaped arrangement using *Spathoglottis* and *Epidendrum*

Example of cut-flower arrangement

For cut-flower production, the programme produces hybrids of *Dendrobium, Arachnis, Aranda, Mokara, Aranthera, Renantanda* and *Oncidium* with the following objectives set for their selection:

- free flowering —new hybrids should be able to produce at least 10 good sprays per year, per plant, in order to be profitable.
- clear and clean-coloured flowers — as major importers for Singapore orchids, Japan and Europe have a high preference for flowers with good colour clarity, and preferably in pastel blue, soft pinks, yellow, white and red.
- fast growing and early flowering — because orchids are relatively slow growers, they are less economical for farmers to cultivate since the returns are being realised far later than most crops. Here the Gardens concentrates on making hybrids that flower within 18 months from the planting of seedlings, thus making orchid growing more financially attractive for farmers.
- disease resistance — the new hybrids should be resistant to most of the major diseases, in order to reduce maintenance work as well as the use of noxious chemicals.
- long flower stem — for the purpose of flower arrangement, a spray cum stalk ratio of 3:1 is ideal.
- good flower size, shape and presentation — depending on the occasion, flower arrangement artists prefer a wide selection of flowers of different genera, sizes, and shapes. Quite often, upright flowers that are round or intermediate in shape are preferred.
- light and compact spray — because orchids are highly perishable, they need to be transported by air, and this represents a major portion of the export cost. Thus the Gardens works towards producing flowers that are light and easy to pack.
- absence of premature fading of flower buds — quality is judged, in part, on the ability of the first flower to stay fresh until the last one opens. This is especially important for flowers with a long spray.
- long vase life — even though many orchid genera are known for their long vase life, the aim is to ensure that cut flowers bred by the Gardens stay fresh for at least 14 days after harvesting.

From the late 60s, in order to make way for industrial development, more people moved to high-rise apartments. Many had to abandon large garden plants for smaller ones suitable for growing in narrow confines. Mindful of the changing needs of the public, the Singapore Botanic Gardens also included the breeding of compact pot-plants in its hybridisation programme.

For home gardening use, hybrids of *Dendrobium, Ascocenda, Mokara, Vandaenopsis, Renanthopsis, Renantanda*, strap-leaved vanda, *Vascostylis* and many other intergeneric hybrids are used. These must possess:

- attractive new colours and colour combinations — hobbyists usually demand novel colours and shapes.
- perfection of bloom — flowers of new hybrids must have better colour, substance, size and shape as judged against others in their own classes.
- lasting flowers — flowers must be able to last for at least two weeks on the plant. Some hybrids have flowers that last for months on the plant.
- free-flowering — plants bred for apartment growing must be able to flower freely under a lower light intensity.
- compactness — with spatial constraints, apartment-dwelling hobbyists prefer plants which can be grown in small pots.
- disease-free — the health of plants is particularly important for those living in apartments as the frequent use of fungicides and insecticides may disturb the neighbours.
- fast growing — the faster a plant grows, the shorter the time it takes from planting to flowering.

The art of orchid hybridisation

The basic principles of orchid breeding are straightforward. However, the production of outstanding hybrids takes plenty of time, dedication, patience, skill, intuition, experience, and last but not least — luck.

After setting out one's breeding objectives, the most critical step is naturally to acquire good stud plants. Proven and potential breeding stocks are usually obtained from nurseries and private collections, and maintaining good relationships with established orchid breeders throughout the world is crucial to getting the 'right' plants.

Once acquired, the stud plants have to be assessed under local conditions. After the plants are established, information such as growth habit and floral and vegetative traits are observed and studied. Only then can the breeder select the best parents and begin with crossing. Once the stud plants are evaluated, the breeder can select the best parents to make the crosses according to the objectives set.

To make the crosses according to plan, one must ensure that both parents flower together. Though some orchids are more free-

Dendrobium Blue Twinkle – an excellent example of a potted plant

A seed pod of a
dendrobium — about
4-5 cm long
Below: Cross section of
an orchid seed,
magnified 100 times

flowering than others, very often both parents do not flower simultaneously. One way to overcome this problem is to store pollinia under low temperatures where orchid pollinia can, under normal circumstances, remain viable for several months. When the stud plant flowers, its pollinia can be stored in the refrigerator. When the second stud plant of a desired cross flowers, pollinia of the first stud can be taken from the refrigerator to make the cross.

When both the parents are ready, artificial pollination begins with the removal of pollinia from the female parent (also known as the pod parent) to prevent self pollination. Pollinia of the male parent are inserted into the stigma of the female parent. To ensure a better chance of success, the cross can be repeated if extra flowers are available. Pollinated flowers are tagged with a label indicating the date of pollination and names of both parents.

After pollination, the seed pods produced are checked regularly so that valuable seeds are not wasted by seed shedding. Depending on the type of plant, seed pods of orchids take about one month to over a year to mature. Upon harvesting, orchid seeds are germinated on a culture media.

Orchid seeds are the smallest among all flowering plants and do not have food-storage cells. They therefore require the presence of a fungus to supply them with nutrients. In 1922, an American scientist, Professor Lewis Knudson, made a breakthrough discovery that profoundly influenced the raising of orchids. He found that the fungus requirement could be by-passed altogether and orchid seeds successfully germinated on a sterile nutrient medium with the addition of sucrose. Then in 1928, Professor Hans Burgeff of Wurzburg introduced the method to Holttum, who applied it to the germination of seeds of his first cross. Since then, seed germination on culture media has become a daily routine.

Six months to a year after germination, the seedlings are ready to be transplanted out of flasks. Firstly, a handful of seedlings is planted in community pots. When the seedlings become established, they are separated, and each seedling planted into a thumb pot. In a few months' time, as the seedlings become larger, they are again transplanted, this time into four to six-inch pots. Very soon, the young plants start to flower, still growing in these pots.

The time taken from unflasking to flowering varies from within a year (as in *Spathoglottis*) to four years (as in some vandas). However, before flowering, inferior or less than hardy seedlings are rigorously culled as they are unlikely to yield successful results. Once flowers appear, new hybrids are visually assessed for colour, shape and arrangement, and only the best are kept for further evaluation. Records on the growth habit and vegetative and floral structures of each of the selected plants are carefully kept. In order to realise the potential of a new hybrid, the plant requires observation for at least a year.

If the selected plant meets all the criteria of a good hybrid, the plant is propagated by tissue culture for a large-scale field trial. The growing point (meristem) of a new shoot is excised from the plant and grown in a culture medium under artificial light at 25°C. Soon, numerous protocorm-like bodies appear, and these eventually become plantlets. Depending on the hybrid, this process of tissue culture, also known as meristeming, takes from one to two years.

To make sure that the quality of the new hybrid is not compromised, the breeder makes a further assessment by growing a few hundred of the tissue-cultured plants. This process allows the breeder to check whether mutation has occurred during tissue culture. Once the new hybrid is proven to be superior to the existing varieties, the next step is to undertake mass propagation by meristeming, followed by large-scale planting.

A new orchid hybrid can be given a name and registered with the Royal Horticultural Society. As of today, the Singapore Botanic Gardens has registered more than 300 hybrids, many of which were named after VIPs who visited the Gardens over the years. Amongst the more famous names are *Dendrobium* Elizabeth (named after Queen Elizabeth of England); *Dendrobium* Margaret Thatcher (named after the former Prime Minister of the United Kingdom); *Aranda* Barbara Bush (named after the wife of Mr. George Bush, former President of the United States of America); and *Renantanda* Akihito (named after Emperor Akihito of Japan).

Top: Six month-old seedlings growing in culture media will eventually be planted in community pots (below).

To make a new hybrid, the breeder needs to overcome many hurdles. One of these is the loss of fertility in the more advanced hybrids. As orchid hybrids become more and more complex, they tend to be less fertile and this results in a reduction in the number of successful crosses. A study of the percentage of successful crosses made in the Singapore Botanic Gardens shows that, from 1983 to 1993, out of all the dendrobium crosses made during that period, 25.1% formed pods, and seeds

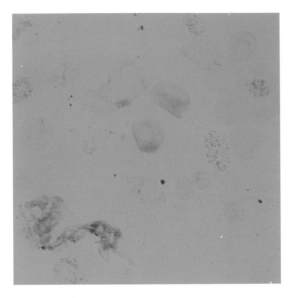

Cytological studies are regularly conducted on the Gardens' hybrids.

from only half of these pods germinated. Where the vandaceous plants are concerned, 19.2% of the crosses set pod and only 3.5% eventually germinated; from those that germinated, only a handful among the best were selected for naming and registration.

In order to breed plants that grow well under the tropical lowland climate, the Singapore Botanic Gardens has been concentrating on the breeding of vandaceous and dendrobium hybrids, both of which are native to the region. These hybrids are free-flowering and grow well under local conditions. The breeding programme also includes some hybrids of *Spathoglottis* and a small number of novel hybrids of other genera.

Vandaceous hybrids

There are numerous genera in this group but the most showy ones are *Aerides, Arachnis, Ascocentrum, Doritis, Paraphalaenopsis, Phalaenopsis, Renanthera, Rhynchostylis,* *Trichoglottis, Vanda* and *Vandopsis.* Most of the hybrids created by the Gardens come from the species of these genera.

Orchids belonging to this group are relatively easy to breed because its members can tolerate a high degree of interspecific and intergeneric breeding. In order to combine the most desirable traits from different plants, breeders work not only within a genus but also between genera. For example, species of *Arachnis* can be crossed with *Vanda* to produce *Aranda* hybrids. When *Arachnis* is crossed with *Renanthera, Aranthera* is formed. Hybrids can be crossed again with other species or hybrids, within the same genus, or between genera to form more complex hybrids. Furthermore, a bigeneric hybrid can be crossed again with a third genus to make a trigeneric hybrid. For example, when *Aranda* Hilda Galistan was crossed with *Renanthera coccinea*, a trigeneric hybrid *Holttumara* Cochineal was created.

Since the beginning of the breeding programme in 1928, the Singapore Botanic Gardens has produced some 170 vandaceous hybrids with representatives from the following genera: *Arachnis, Aranda, Aranthera, Aeridovanda, Renantanda, Vanda, Holttumara, Vandaenopsis, Renanthopsis, Chuanyenara, Renanthera, Renanopsis, Ridleyara,* and *Arachnopsis.*

The Singapore Botanic Gardens is credited with creating the new genera of *Holttumara, Ridleyara* and *Arachnoglottis. Holttumara* Cochineal is the first trigeneric hybrid between *Vanda, Arachnis* and *Renanthera; Ridleyara* Fascad is the first hybrid between *Vanda, Arachnis* and *Trichoglottis;* and *Arachnoglottis* Brown Bars is the first bigeneric hybrid between *Arachnis* and *Trichoglottis.*

Dendrobium hybrids

The genus *Dendrobium* is the second largest in the world next to *Bulbophyllum.* It is also the single genus which has the most hybrids made by the Singapore Botanic Gardens. Since the 1940 registration of *Dendrobium* Helen Park, the first *Dendrobium* hybrid of the Singapore Botanic Gardens, the breeding programme has produced more than 120 registered hybrids of this genus.

There are many sections within the genus *Dendrobium.* As far as horticultural interest is concerned, the sections *Spatulata, Phalaenanthe, Dendrobium* and *Latouria* are the most important. In Singapore, because species belonging to section *Spatulata* and *Phalaenanthe* flower well, most hybrids are made by using plants from these two sections.

The *Spatulata* section consists of plants which are also known as the an-telope or the horn-type orchids, so named because their twisted petals resemble the horns of an antelope. Most of them have origins in the Pacific region such as Papua New Guinea, Celebes, Sunda Islands, Queensland (Australia) and the Philippines. Some of the more popular species include *Dendrobium gouldii, D. schulleri, D. lineale, D. mirbelianum, D. nindii, D. lasianthera, D. stratiotes, D. discolor, D. johannis, D. tangerinum, D. antennatum,* and *D. taurinum.* Because these species flower well in the tropical lowlands and produce lasting blooms, they make ideal plants for growing in the tropics.

In comparison to the *Spatulata* dendrobiums, species belonging to the section *Phalaenanthe* have broad

Dendrobium Singa Mas – a recent product of the breeding programme and a potential cut-flower hybrid

petals and sepals. Typical species of this section are *Dendrobium phalaenopsis, D. biggibum* and *D. dicuphum*. They are natives of Australia's Queensland, Papua New Guinea and Indonesia. Even though these species have rounder flowers, they are not as lasting and free-flowering as the spatulatas.

To combine the good traits from various plants, crosses can be made within and between sections. For example, when crosses are made between species of the sections *Spatulata* and *Phalaenanthe*, intermediate-type dendrobiums are formed, so called because their flowers are of an intermediate shape between the spatulatas and the phalaenanthes. These hybrids are very vigorous, free-flowering, colourful, and they have longer sprays and lasting flowers.

As you will see in the following pages, the Singapore Botanic Gardens is well-known for breeding *Spatulata* and intermediate types of dendrobiums. Many of these hybrids were named after VIPs and several of them are important cut flowers. A large number of them have become excellent landscape plants. In addition, several have been used extensively as stud plants throughout the world.

Others

Apart from the vandaceous and the dendrobiums, the Singapore Botanic Gardens is also well-known for breeding *Spathoglottis*. As mentioned earlier, the first hybrid Holttum produced was *Spathoglottis* Primrose. Out of some 40 *Spathoglottis* hybrids existing worldwide, nine were created by the Singapore Botanic Gardens. All but one of these were made during Holttum's time.

The breeding of *Spathoglottis* almost stopped after the 1940s due to the loss of valuable breeding stock during the Japanese occupation. From the 1950s onwards, as the breeding programme regained strength, more interest was shown in vandaceous and dendrobium orchids, and the breeding of *Spathoglottis* virtually ceased.

Recently, however, the Singapore Botanic Gardens has renewed its interest in breeding *Spathoglottis* with species such as *Spathoglottis unguiculata, S. kimbaliana* and *S. tomentosa* used as breeding stock. The objectives are to produce compact, free-flowering and more colourful hybrids for landscaping and pot-plant usage. So far, the results have been encouraging.

Other genera with hybrids registered by the Singapore Botanic Gardens include candidates from *Brassidium, Doritaenopsis, Epilaeliocattleya, Laeliocattleya, Oncidium,* and *Paphiopedilum*. For more information on specific hybrids, please refer to the alphabetical listing of selected Singapore Botanic Gardens' orchids described in the appendix.

The Gardens' Hybrids

As at today, the Singapore Botanic Gardens has registered some 300 hybrids. Many of these hybrids are illustrated in the following section. The vandaceous hybrids are featured first, followed by the dendrobiums and the other genera.

Renantanda **Jane McNeill** (*Vanda* B. P. Mok x *Renanthera storiei*). This is one of the most beautiful *Renantanda* hybrids which has V. Miss Joaquim in its background. The upright inflorescence can reach 50 cm in length, bearing 10 to 12 beautiful blooms. The flowers have a pleasant erythrite red with slightly darker spots throughout. The sepals and petals are in harmony with a brightly coloured lip, chrysanthemum crimson on its apical half and cadmium orange at the throat.

Vandaceous Hybrids

***Aeridovanda* Jehan El Sadat** (*Vanda* Trisum x *Aerides odorata*). This lovely monopodial carries inflorescences 25 to 30 cm in length, bearing 12 to 20 well-arranged flowers. Flowers measure 4.5 cm across. The petals and sepals are pastel mauve with light mineral-violet edges and are marked with light erythrite-red spots. The lip is naples yellow with erythrite-red spots. This beautiful plant grows well in partial shade and was named after Jehan El Sadat, the wife of the former President of Egypt, Anwar Sadat, in 1977.

***Arachnis* Ishbel** (*Arachnis maingayi* x *Arachnis hookeriana*) is the first *Arachnis* hybrid produced by the Singapore Botanic Gardens. The 30 to 40-cm-long inflorescences bear 6 to 8 flowers, each 7 cm across. The sepals and petals are pure white with bright purple markings; they are accompanied by a bright purple lip. Although it is not as robust as *Arachnis* Maggie Oei, this free-flowering hybrid has been used extensively for hybridisation. Some of its outstanding progeny are *Mokara* Khaw Phaik Suan, *Aranda* Lily Chong and *Aranthera* Beatrice Ng.

***Arachnoglottis* Brown Bars** (*Arachnis* Maggie Oei x *Trichoglottis fasciata*). *Arachnoglottis* is an artificial genus created by crossing *Arachnis* and *Trichoglottis*. *Arachnoglottis* Brown Bars is the first hybrid of this genus in the world. This beautiful hybrid bears characteristics of both its parents. The branching inflorescences reach a length of 80 to 100 cm, with 20 to 30 well-spaced flowers. Individual star-shaped flowers are 6.5 cm across. The petals and sepals are light yellow with many distinct reddish brown bars. The fleshy lip is yellow and its throat is brown. So far, *Arachnoglottis* Brown Bars has only produced one hybrid, *Irvingara* Encik Peh (*Arachnoglottis* Brown Bars x *Renanthera storiei*).

***Arachnopsis* Eric Holttum** (*Arachnis* Maggie Oei x *Paraphalaenopsis denevei*) was named after Professor Eric Holttum, the founder of the breeding programme in the Singapore Botanic Gardens. This semi-terete hybrid carries compact sprays about 15 to 20 cm in length. Each spray displays 6 to 9 flowers which are 7 cm across. The most beautiful variety among all the seedlings is 'Barred Beauty'. The sepals and petals have a yellow background with red bars and spots. The midlobe of the lip is scarlet whereas the throat and the lateral-lobes are yellow with streaks of red. *Arachnopsis* Eric Holttum in turn has produced several beautiful hybrids. Some examples are *Sappanara* Ahmad Zahab (*Arachnopsis* Eric Holttum x *Renanthera storiei*) and *Bokchoonara* Khaw Bian Huat (*Arachnopsis* Eric Holttum x *Ascocenda* Tan Chai Beng).

***Aranda* Bertha Braga** (*Vanda tricolor* x *Arachnis* Maggie Oei) was originated by A. J. Braga and registered by the Singapore Botanic Gardens. The inflorescences vary in length from 25 to 40 cm, bearing up to 14 flowers. The spider-shaped flowers are about 9 cm across, yellow to greenish yellow, with purple-brown spots; the lateral-lobes of the lip are dark pink with some mauve streaks and the mid-lobe is purple. This lovely hybrid is still being exported from Singapore.

***Aranda* Belzonica** (*Arachnis* Ishbel x *Vanda luzonica*) is a free-flowering plant, with inflorescences reaching 40 cm in length bearing more than 15 flowers on each. The flowers, which are well displayed, measure about 7 cm across. The hybrid inherited the scorpion shape from its *Arachnis* parent and the colour from the *Vanda* parent. The white sepals are spotted or flushed in purple, the intensity of which increases towards the tips. This hybrid which grows under full sun was once a popular cut flower.

Aranda Eric Mekie (*Aranda* Lucy Laycock x *Vanda luzonica*). This beautiful plant looks very similar to its female parent except for the broader petals and sepals, as well as the less intense purplish splash. The upright sprays of this lovely hybrid are 40 cm in length, bearing 12 to 15 well-spaced flowers. Each flower is 6 cm across. The white sepals and petals are flushed in petunia purple, with purple spots and tessellations. The mid-lobe of the lip is petunia purple and it is complemented by the white, faintly spotted lateral-lobes.

Aranda Deborah (*Arachnis hookeriana* x *Vanda lamellata*) was the first *Aranda* raised in the Singapore Botanic Gardens. It was named after the daughter of Professor Eric Holttum. This vigorous plant bears 40 to 50-cm-long sprays with up to 14 flowers on each. Each flower is 5 cm across. Like *Vanda lamellata*, the sepals and petals are cream with irregular spots and streaks of purple; they are accompanied by a purple lip. The sun-loving plant was once a popular cut flower in the 1950s and 1960s.

Aranda Hilda Galistan (*Arachnis hookeriana* x *Vanda tricolor* var. *suavis*) is a beautiful primary hybrid originated in the early 1940s. The 40 to 45-cm-long inflorescence bears 8 to 10 well-displayed, fragrant flowers. Each flower is 6 cm across. There are several clones of the hybrid. The basal colour of the petals and sepals varies from cream to light mauve with crimson spots. Because of its attractive appearance and fragrance, this charming hybrid has been used as a cut flower from the 1950s up until today.

Aranda Grandeur (*Arachnis flosaeris* x *Vanda* Ellen Noa) was considered one of the most handsome arandas in the 1960s because of its sizeable flowers and showy colour. Each 35 to 40-cm-long inflorescence bears 8 to 10 large blooms. Each flower is 11 cm across, rather large for an aranda. The basal colour of the sepals and petals is yellow; they are subtly speckled with maroon spots and are flushed light red towards the tips. The Malayan Orchid Society presented an Award of Merit to the variety 'Hitam' in 1962.

***Aranda* Majula** (*Arachnis* Maggie Oei x *Vanda insignis*). The upright inflorescence of this beautiful hybrid can reach 50 cm in length, bearing more than 10 well-arranged flowers. Each waxy flower is 7.5 cm across. The attractive petals and sepals are sulphur yellow with ruby-red blotches. The relatively broad lip, which is inherited from the male parent, is mineral violet and finely spotted with ruby red. The white column provides a good contrast to the rest of the flower. The Orchid Society of South East Asia awarded an H.C.C. to the variety 'Rimau', and in 1993 it won a White Ribbon at the 14th World Orchid Conference in Glasgow.

***Aranda* Nancy O'Neil** (*Arachnis hookeriana* x *Vanda* Harvest Time) The hybrid carries an erect inflorescence measuring 40 cm long, with 6 to 9 flowers. The fragrant flowers measure 7.5 cm across. The petals and sepals are cream yellow with erythrite-red spots. This VIP orchid was named after Mrs. Nancy O'Neil, the wife of the former Deputy Prime Minister of West Australia, in 1977.

Aranthera **Anne Black** (*Arachnis* Maggie Oei x *Renanthera coccinea*). This is the first VIP orchid of the Singapore Botanic Gardens. It was named after Lady Black, the wife of the former Governor of Singapore, Sir Robert Black, in 1957. The vigorous plant bears branching inflorescences that reach 80 cm in length, with more than 40 well-displayed flowers. Individual flowers are 5.3 cm across. The sepals and petals are scarlet with some dark crimson bars. Being one of the few fertile arantheras, *Aranthera* Anne Black has produced 7 hybrids.

Aranda **Peter Ewart** (*Arachnis hookeriana* var. *luteola* x *Vanda* Kapoho). This free flowering hybrid bears sprays measuring 40 to 45 cm long with some 15 well-arranged flowers. Individual flowers are 6.5 cm across. The sepals and petals are dark empire yellow with streaks and spots of crimson lake which intensify towards the tips; they are accompanied by an orchid-purple lip which has a white throat. This vigorous hybrid was a very popular cut-flower plant in the 1960s.

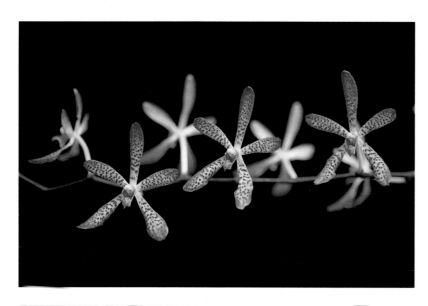

Aranthera **Dainty** (*Arachnis hookeriana* var. *luteola* x *Renanthera monachica*). A vigorous plant of this beautiful primary hybrid bears branching sprays some 60 cm in length, with 20 to 25 well-spaced flowers. Individual flowers are 4 cm across. Unlike most arantheras which are crimson in colour, the flowers of *Aranthera* Dainty are of a light orange-red with crimson spots. The Malayan Orchid Society presented an Award of Merit to the clone 'Prolific' in 1958.

Aranthera **James Storie** (*Arachnis hookeriana* x *Renanthera storiei*) was one of the earliest hybrids brought to flower by the Singapore Botanic Gardens, as well as the first *Aranthera* hybrid registered. The hybrid was named after James Storie, who first discovered the male parent, *Renanthera storiei*. The branching inflorescence is about 50 to 60 cm long, with some 20 flowers. The 4.5-cm-wide flowers are dark crimson with some darker markings and have a velvety texture. Six hybrids have resulted from this fertile *Aranthera*.

Ascocenda **Iris Harris** (*Vanda* Wee Kim Lian x *Ascocentrum curvifolium*). This lovely hybrid is one of the two ascocendas registered by the Singapore Botanic Gardens. The waxy flowers are arranged symmetrically around the 20-cm-long inflorescence. Individual flowers are 3.1 cm across. The orange petals and sepals are spotted with red. They are complemented by a yellow lip with some red stripes. Whereas *Vanda* Wee Kim Lian passed on the texture to its progeny, *Ascocentrum curvifolium* transmitted the colour and increased the number of flowers. The showy plant grows well on stumps. It flowers freely and the blooms last for a long time.

Ascocenda **Singa Chiba** (*Vanda* Josephine van Brero x *Ascocenda* David Parker). This recent hybrid of the Singapore Botanic Gardens was named after Chiba Botanic Gardens, our Sister Gardens in Japan. The plant inherited the best traits from both parents. Its famous mother, *Vanda* Josephine van Brero, imparted the excellent substance and the showy lip, and the male parent passed on the form and floriferousness. The free-flowering plant bears upright sprays with up to 10 spirally-arranged flowers. The natural spread of the flower is 7.3 cm across.

Christieara Ramiah (*Ascocenda* Mang-kiatkul x *Aerides odorata*). *Christieara* is an artificial genus which consists of *Aerides, Ascocentrum* and *Vanda*. Each spray of this showy hybrid bears many compactly arranged flowers. The sub-erect inflorescence gradually becomes pendulous when all the blooms are fully opened. The flowers range from 5 to 6 cm across. The colour of individual flowers varies from light pink to orange red to bright red, with some spots. *Christieara* Ramiah was named to honour a gardener, Muthiya Pillai Ramiah, who worked for more than 50 years in the Gardens' orchid nursery.

Chuanyenara Mei-Tsung (*Renanstylis* Queen Emma x *Arachnis hookeriana*). This free-flowering hybrid produces an upright and branching inflorescence that bears numerous attractive flowers. The natural spread of the flower is 4.6 cm across. The flower is purplish pink with beetroot-purple spots. The white lip is adorned with beetroot-purple spots and splashes. This VIP orchid was named after the wife of the former Prime Minister of the Republic of China, Mr. Yu Kuo Hwa, in 1987.

Doritaenopsis **Elizabeth Waldheim** (*Doritis pulcherrima* x *Phalaenopsis* Lam Soon). A robust plant of this free-flowering hybrid bears 90-cm-long inflorescences with some 30 charming flowers. Each flower measures 4.2 cm across. The petals and sepals are a pleasing pastel violet-pink which becomes darker towards the base. The lip's mid-lobe is slightly darker than the rest of the flower. This beautiful orchid was named after the wife of the former Secretary General of the United Nations, Dr. Kurt Waldheim, in 1980.

Holttumara **Cochineal** (*Aranda* Hilda Galistan 'Suntan' x *Renanthera coccinea*). This is the first trigeneric hybrid made up of the genera *Vanda, Arachnis* and *Renanthera*. The branching inflorescence can reach half a meter long, bearing 35 to 40 flowers. The flowers are 3.5 cm across and are of good substance. Like most hybrids of renantheras, the dominant colour of the petals and sepals is red with a tinge of orange. The plant flowers well under full sun. The artificial genus was named to honour Professor R. E. Holttum for pioneering orchid hybridisation in the Singapore Botanic Gardens.

***Phalaenopsis* Barbara Bush** (*Phalaenopsis* Best Girl x *Phalaenopsis* Shim Beauty). This graceful hybrid bears 60 to 65-cm-long inflorescences which hang down naturally, displaying 8 to 10 symmetrically arranged flowers. Individual flowers measure 9 cm across and are of good substance. The purplish pink sepals and petals are accompanied by a reddish purple lip with a tinge of orange yellow. This lovely hybrid grows well under semi-shade and flowers twice a year. This first *Phalaenopsis* hybrid of the Singapore Botanic Gardens was named after the wife of Mr. George Bush, former President of the United States, during their visit to Singapore in 1992.

***Renantanda* Akihito** (*Vanda* Manila x *Renanthera coccinea*). *Renantanda* is an artificial genus created by crossing *Vanda* and *Renanthera*. A mature plant of this hybrid can bear sprays over 70 cm in length, each carrying more than 20 well-spaced blooms. The shape of the flower resembles that of the male parent. Each flower is 6.2 cm across. The narrow and long dorsal sepal is slightly twisted and the broad lateral sepals sometimes overlap each other. The colour of the flower is a rare currant red. This handsome plant grows well under full sun. The plant was named in honour of Emperor Akihito of Japan during his visit to the Singapore Botanic Gardens in 1970.

***Renantanda* Hannelore Schmidt** (*Vanda* Wee Kim Lian x *Renanthera philippinensis*). This handsome plant carries erect and branching inflorescences up to 45 cm in length. Each spray bears more than 60 flowers of good substance. The natural spread of the flower is 4 cm across. The basal colour of the petals and sepals is yellow and is heavily flushed with a deep burnt orange; the base is spotted further with chrysanthemum crimson. A distinctive yellow edge is found around all floral parts. This showy plant was named after the wife of Mr. Helmut Schmidt, former Chancellor of the Federal Republic of Germany, in 1979.

***Renantanda* Keating** (*Renanthera* Jessie Loke x *Vanda* Siti Zain). This handsome hybrid bears 28 to 35-cm-long horizontal spikes, with over 30 well-arranged flowers. The flowers are 5.5 cm across. The orange sepals and petals are densely spotted in dark orange red. They are further embellished by a beautiful lip, the mid-lobe of which is yellow orange and the lateral-lobes are white with red spots. The variety 'Annita' of this brilliant hybrid was named in 1993 after the wife of the Prime Minister of Australia, Mr. Paul Keating.

Renantanda **Mary Robinson** (*Vanda* Nellie Morley x *Renanthera* Tom Story). One of the latest and most brilliantly coloured hybrids of the Singapore Botanic Gardens, this handsome plant bears upright sprays 35 to 44 cm in length, with 8 to 12 well-arranged flowers. The flowers are 9 cm across. The radiantly coloured petals and sepals have an orange background with red spots. They are further adorned by a matching lip with a purple mid-lobe and spotted lateral-lobes. The plant was named in 1993 after Mrs. Mary Robinson, Prime Minister of the Republic of Ireland.

Renantanda **Prince Norodom Sihanouk** (*Vanda* Tan Chay Yan x *Renanthera coccinea*). This beautiful hybrid inherited the features which characterize both its famous parents. The 50 to 60-cm-long, branching inflorescences bear numerous flowers 4.5 cm wide. The petals and sepals are orange red except for some spots on the lateral sepals. The yellow lateral-lobes are spotted with red, and the pointed mid-lobe is crimson with two bright yellow keels. This handsome hybrid was named in honour of Prince Norodom Sihanouk of Cambodia during his visit to the Singapore Botanic Gardens in 1962.

***Renanthera* Rattanakosin** (*Renanthera matutina* x *Renanthera philippinensis*). An interesting primary hybrid between two renantheras, this plant carries branching sprays 70 to 85 cm in length that display up to 180 flowers. Each flower is 4.7 cm tall and 1.5 cm across. The sepals and petals are a fiery orange red and densely covered with deep red blotches. The striking hybrid was named to commemorate Bangkok's Bicentennial in 1982.

***Renanthopsis* Dhanabalan** (*Renanthopsis* Yee Peng x *Renanthera* Kalsom). This handsome plant bears 20 to 30-cm-long horizontal spikes with an average of 25 nicely displayed flowers. The star-shaped flowers are 5.7 cm across. The orange petals are complemented beautifully by the orange-red sepals. The red mid-lobe of the lip is adorned by a yellow-orange throat that is spotted in dark red. This orchid was named after Mr. S. Dhanabalan, the former Minister of National Development of Singapore.

***Ridleyara* Fascad** (*Aranda* Eileen Addison x *Trichoglottis fasciata*). The first trigeneric hybrid with *Arachnis, Vanda* and *Trichoglottis* in its background, this unusual plant bears inflorescences that can reach a length of 50 cm, bearing up to 14 flowers. Each flower is 7 cm across; the petals and sepals are yellow with brown spots which intensify towards the tips. To date, this plant is still the only registered hybrid of the artificial genus. The new genus was named after a former Director of the Singapore Botanic Gardens, Mr. H. N. Ridley.

***Vanda* Bellasan** (*Vanda* Rubella x *Vanda sanderiana*). This fifth-generation hybrid of *Vanda* Miss Joaquim is very attractive and free flowering. The semi-terete plant bears upright inflorescences 35 to 40 cm in length with 10 to 12 showy flowers. The flowers are 6.5 cm across. The dorsal sepal and petals are petunia purple with a faint flush of cream and darker petunia-purple venation towards the centre. The lateral sepals are similarly coloured except for a tinge of yellow. They are contrasted by a dark purple lip.

***Vanda* Farah Pahlavi** (*Vanda* Ling x *Vanda tessellata*). An unusual-coloured hybrid, this strap-leafed *Vanda* bears some 20-cm-long inflorescences with 6 to 8 blooms on each. The natural spread of the flower is 4.7 cm across, and its texture is excellent. The sepals and petals are mimosa yellow with red-brown spots throughout; the apical half is flushed light purple. The mid-lobe of the lip is moorish blue, and the white lateral-lobes are finely spotted in the same colour as the mid-lobe. This orchid was named after the former Empress Farah Pahlavi of Iran in 1974.

***Vanda* Memoria Alex Donald** (*Vanda* Josephine van Brero x *Vanda* Prolific). A graceful hybrid produced in the 1950s, this beautiful hybrid bears inflorescences 30 cm in length with 8 to 10 brightly coloured flowers. Each flower is 8 cm across. The dorsal sepal and petals are light orchid purple with slightly darker spots, except that the lower half of the lateral sepals is yellow. This hybrid inherited the characteristic lip from the female parent; the crimson purple at the mid-lobe gradually changes to a bright mauve towards the apex; the lateral-lobes are bright yellow with crimson spots.

Vanda Norbert Alphonso (*Vanda* Alice Laycock x *Vanda* Cooperi). This semi-terete *Vanda* has inflorescences 30 to 40 cm in length, bearing over 10 lovely flowers. Individual flowers are 6.5 cm across. The flower is dominated by its outstanding scarlet-purple lip which creates a good contrast to the light purple petals and sepals. When the flowers first open, the lip is flat but curls downwards after a few days. The plant is free flowering and grows well under full sun. This beautiful hybrid was named after the son of Mr. George Alphonso, the former Acting Director of the Singapore Botanic Gardens (1970-76).

***Vanda* Prolific** (*Vanda* Nam Kee x *Vanda* Singapore). This terete *Vanda* shows a marked improvement over all its ancestors in terms of texture, shape and colour. It begins to flower when the plant is less than a metre tall. The plant bears inflorescences about 30 cm in length with 3 to 6 flowers of good substance. The dorsal sepal and petals are orchid purple, and the lateral sepals are lighter in colour. The most attractive feature is the well-spread scarlet purple lip. Being free flowering and a short bloomer, this is an excellent plant for landscaping.

***Vanda* Rubella** (*Vanda* Ruby x *Vanda* Prolific). A well-grown plant of this semi-terete hybrid can carry inflorescences 30 cm long with some 10 beautiful blooms. The flowers are 6.5 cm across. The sepals and petals are pale orchid purple with darker purple spots. Like its parents, this hybrid is dominated by its magnificent broad, showy lip; the mid-lobe is about 4 cm wide and dark crimson purple with darker spots. The flower of *Vanda* Rubella is very similar to *Vanda* Ruby Prince, except that the former has a bigger lip and a better form.

Vanda **Sanada Kuma** (*Vanda* B. P. Mok 'Old Rose' x *Vanda* Bill Sutton). This attractive quarter-terete hybrid bears erect inflorescences with some 10 to 15 well-arranged flowers. The flowers are of good substance, each measuring 8 cm across. The sepals and petals are phlox purple with darker tessellations; they are accompanied by a brick-red lip with an amber yellow throat. The plant grows and flowers freely under full sun.

Vanda **Singa Joaquim Centenary** (*Vanda* Josephine van Brero x *Vanda* Miss Joaquim). The spirally-arranged flowers of this semi-terete *Vanda* are borne on its erect, 13-cm-long spike. The eye-catching flowers are 6.6 cm across. The dorsal sepal and the petals are a soothing pastel red with brighter red purple veins. The upper half of the lateral sepals has a pastel red shade, and the lower half is peach orange. The most prominent feature of the flower is the lip; the scarlet mid-lobe is spotted red and the lateral-lobes are yellow orange. This beautiful hybrid was named in 1993 to commemorate the 100th birthday of *Vanda* Miss Joaquim.

Vanda **Wong Poh Nee** (*Vanda* Josephine van Brero x *Vanda tessellata*). A hybrid of the early 1960s, this *Vanda* has a 30-cm-long inflorescence that can carry up to 10 flowers. Each flower is 6.7 cm across. Unlike most hybrids of *Vanda* Josephine van Brero which are peach or orange red, the colour of the flowers of this hybrid is intermediate between the parents. The sepals and petals are yellow ochre with a faint flush of violet and slightly darker tessellations and spots. The lip takes on the form of a typical hybrid of the female parent; the mid-lobe is erythrite red and spotted throughout in darker violet.

Vandaenopsis **Sisir** (*Vanda* Wee Kim Lian x *Paraphalaenopsis denevei*) A semi-terete hybrid, the plant bears lovely, spirally-arranged flowers on the 30-cm-long inflorescence. Individual flowers are 6 cm across. The sepals and petals have a basal colour of white with a tinge of grey; they are further spotted with some purplish brown spots. The protruding bright orange brown lip provides a good complement to the rest of the flower. This elegant hybrid was named after the Singapore Institute of Standards and Industrial Research (SISIR).

***Vandaenopsis* Leo Tan** (*Vandaenopsis* Prosperitas x *Vanda* Kultana Gold). This interesting quarter-terete hybrid carries inflorescences 20 to 25 cm in length, with some 10 flowers, each 8 cm across. The flowers have a very unusual light yellow brown colour throughout, contrasted by the white column. This fine hybrid was named after Professor Leo Tan, a former Member of the National Parks Board.

Dendrobium Hybrids

***Dendrobium* Asean Beauty** (*Dendrobium* Garnet Beauty x *Dendrobium* Pink Lips). This magnificent semi-cane type *Dendrobium* carries sprays 40 to 50 cm in length with more than 20 well-arranged flowers. The attractive, intermediate-shaped flowers are 7.5 cm across. The slightly curled sepals and petals have a peach glow on a yellow background gradually turning light yellow toward the base. The light purple lip is complemented by a clear yellow throat. *Dendrobium* Asean Beauty was named to commemorate the ASEAN Summit which took place in Singapore in 1992.

Dendrobium Elizabeth (*Dendrobium* Mustard x *Dendrobium* Noor Aishah). The majestic cane-type *Dendrobium* carries 35 to 45-cm-long inflorescences with 25 to 30 well-arranged blooms. The flowers are of good substance, each measuring 5.5 cm across. The twisted petals and the sepals are Dresden yellow with light greyish purple streaks, accompanied by a graceful lip that is uranium green flushed with greyish purple. This beautiful hybrid was named after Queen Elizabeth II of the United Kingdom during her visit to the Singapore Botanic Gardens in 1972.

Dendrobium De Klerk (*Dendrobium* Mari Michener x *Dendrobium* Lena Jansen) is a semi-cane type *Dendrobium* with sprays 50 to 65 cm in length, displaying some 20 spirally-arranged flowers. Each intermediate-shaped flower measures 6.6 cm across. The floral parts are yellow green with purple venations which become intensified on the lip. The VIP orchid was named after Mr. F. W. De Klerk, former President of the Republic of South Africa, during his visit to the Singapore Botanic Gardens in 1992.

***Dendrobium* Gloria Lim** (*Dendrobium* Ekapol x *Dendrobium* Sharifah Fatimah) carries semi-erect spikes that are 40 to 50-cm-long, bearing an average of 15 flowers. The round, good-textured flowers are 6.5 cm across. There are variations in the colour of the flowers among the offspring. The more outstanding clones have white or light yellow floral parts that are adorned with a flush of orchid purple. The lip is white or yellow at the throat and gradually becomes orchid purple towards the apex. This vigorous hybrid was named after Professor Gloria Lim, a Member of the National Parks Board.

***Dendrobium* Iwen Tan** (*Dendrobium helix* x *Dendrobium* Madame Uraiwan). This is a handsome bicolour hybrid that has some 50-cm-long, upright sprays which carry 25 to 30 spirally-arranged flowers. The intermediate-shaped flowers are of good substance, each measuring 5.8 cm across. The yellow sepals and petals, which are slightly curled, contrast against the showy greyish-purple lip. The exotic-looking hybrid was named after Mrs. Iwen Tan, the wife of the Chairman of the National Parks Board.

Dendrobium Jane Denny (_Dendrobium_ Jennie Ang x _Dendrobium_ Fran's Jewel). This compact hybrid carries 50 to 60-cm-long arching sprays with more than 15 well-spaced flowers on each. Individual flowers are some 5 cm across; the sepals and petals are an unusual violet blue, which was inherited from both parents. This hybrid was named after Australian Jane Denny, the 4 millionth visitor to Singapore in 1989.

Dendrobium John Nauen (_Dendrobium_ formosum x _Dendrobium_ ovipositoriferum). Like its parents, this hybrid bears short inflorescences with 2 to 5 flowers, each measuring 6 cm across. The attractive, pure white flowers resemble the female parent, except that the progeny have a better form and are enriched by an orange-yellow lip throat. This hybrid was named after John Charles Nauen, the first Assistant Curator of the orchid nursery who served from 1935 until 1942.

Dendrobium **Khunying Boonruen**
(*Dendrobium* Sirima Bandaranaike x *Dendrobium* Pink Lips) is one of the Gardens' best antelope dendrobiums which bears numerous sprays that are 50 cm long, each displaying more than 40 spirally-arranged flowers. The colour of the flowers varies considerably from pastel pink to orchid purple. The vigorous plant blooms throughout the year when grown under full sun. During the peak flowering seasons, each plant can bear more than 10 upright sprays. This superior hybrid won two major trophies in thc 1990 Orchid Society of South East Asia (OSSEA) Orchid Show. They were the John Laycock Challenge Cup for the best local hybrid and the Quek Kiah Huat Challenge Cup for the best local *Dendrobium*. This VIP orchid was named after the wife of Maj-Gen Chatichai Choonhavan, the former Prime Minister of Thailand, on their visit to the Singapore Botanic Gardens in 1988.

Dendrobium **Margaret Thatcher**
(*Dendrobium* Concham x *Dendrobium lasianthera*). This well-known orchid produces inflorescences 40 to 50 cm in length with more than 50 spirally-arranged flowers. Each of the antelope flowers measures 5 cm across. The sepals are white at the base and gradually become brownish red towards the apex. The horn-like petals are a clear beetroot purple, becoming purplish brown at the ends. The petals and sepals are accompanied by a dark pink lip. The orchid was named after Baroness Margaret Thatcher, former Prime Minister of the United Kingdom, during her visit to the Singapore Botanic Gardens in 1985.

Dendrobium Masako Kotaishi Hidenka
(*Dendrobium* Singa Snow x *Dendrobium* Subang). This plant's habit is compact and vigorous. Multiple sprays of flowers can reach 50 cm in length, each bearing some 20 well-arranged flowers. The flowers are bright white with a faint blush in the throat. This elegant *Dendrobium* hybrid was named in honour of Princess Masako of Japan, to commemorate the royal wedding with Prince Naruhito in 1993.

Dendrobium **Michiko** (*Dendrobium* Concham x *Dendrobium* Noor Aishah). The compact canes of this *Dendrobium* hybrid beautifully set off the numerous long sprays when in flower. One choice clone 'Princess' has long arching spikes averaging 35 cm in length and bearing some 25 spirally-arranged flowers. Each flower measures 4.5 cm across. The rich chestnut-brown petals contrast beautifully with the bright yellow lip and the sepals. The plant grows well and flowers freely in full sun. This orchid was named in honour of Empress Michiko of Japan during her visit to the Singapore Botanic Gardens in 1970.

Dendrobium **National Parks** (*Dendrobium* Tan Nam Keow x *Dendrobium* Merritt Island). This compact hybrid bears arching inflorescences 60 cm in length, with some 30 gracefully arranged flowers on each. The flower measures 4.8 cm across. There are some variations amongst the seedlings. While the majority are white with pink stripes, several are light green and only a few clones are pure white. This charming hybrid was chosen to represent the National Parks Board when the statutory board was formed in 1990.

Dendrobium Premier Yusof (*Dendrobium nindii* x *Dendrobium* Anita). The cane-like pseudobulbs of this beautiful hybrid bear long, upright sprays with 30 to 35 spirally-arranged flowers. The antelope flowers measure 3 cm across. Flowers of the best clone have dark brown sepals which are matched by the captivating, reddish brown petals and lip. Several outstanding hybrids of the Gardens are the progeny of *Dendrobium* Premier Yusof; two examples are *Dendrobium* Sok Hiong Wee and *Dendrobium* Singa Hyogo. This unique hybrid was named after the First President of Singapore, Tun Yusof bin Ishak.

Dendrobium Ria (*Dendrobium* Mary Trowse x *Dendrobium* Candy Stripe). This is a lovely, compact plant which bears arching sprays 50 to 55 cm in length. Each spray carries up to 25 well-displayed flowers measuring 4.5 cm across. All floral parts have a delicate, slightly wavy appearance. Like the male parent, the basal colour of the flowers is creamy white with attractive dark pink stripes. A few clones resemble the female parent as they are light green with no stripes. The orchid was named in 1991 to honour the wife of the Prime Minister of the Netherlands, Mrs. Ria Lubber Houggeweegan.

Dendrobium **Richard** **Hale** (*Dendrobium* Garnet Beauty x *Dendrobium tangerinum*). This brilliantly coloured hybrid carries inflorescences up to 60 cm in length. A long spike displays more than 50 spectacular flowers. Individual flowers are 5 cm across and the petals curl gracefully. Colours of the flowers vary from currant red to an eye-catching orange. Mr. Richard Hale is a Member of the National Parks Board.

Dendrobium **Ryzhkova** (*Dendrobium* Garnet Beauty x *Dendrobium* Fran's Twist). This vigorous hybrid bears long sprays 50 cm in length, each having an average of 30 flowers. There are considerable variations amongst the seedlings. The flowers of the most beautiful clone measure 6 cm across and are of excellent substance. The slightly curled petals are beetroot purple with an attractive glossy finish; the sepals are a similar colour except for the light yellow area towards the base. They are accompanied by a showy violet-purple lip. The VIP orchid was named after Mrs. Lioudmila Ryzhkova, the wife of the former Prime Minister of the previous Union of the Soviet Socialist Republic in 1990. *Dendrobium* Ryzhkova won a trophy in the 1991 Japan Grand Prix International Orchid Festival for the best *Dendrobium* cut flower of the show.

Dendrobium Singa Dear Mary (*Dendrobium* Mary Trowse x *Dendrobium dearei*). This interesting hybrid consists of species from three different sections in its background, namely *Phalaenanthe, Spatulata* and *Formosae*. The compact pseudobulbs are 30 to 35 cm long. The arching sprays droop gracefully to display the 10 to 11 nicely arranged flowers. The flowers, 4.4 cm across, are white with a slight tinge of green. The long-lasting flowers can stay on the plant for 2 months.

Dendrobium Saleha (*Dendrobium* Mie Fukuda x *Dendrobium* Mary Trowse). This robust and free-flowering hybrid bears 40 to 45-cm-long sprays, with some 25 flowers on each. Individual flowers measure 5 cm across. The slightly twisted petals are golden brown and the sepals are yellow brown; this is further complemented by a showy lip similar in colour to the petals. The VIP orchid was named in 1990 after the wife of the Sultan of Brunei, Hassanah Bolkiah.

***Dendrobium* Singa Mas** (*Dendrobium* Sharifah Fatimah x *Dendrobium* Tan Nam Keow). This attractive plant is one of the most beautiful hybrids created by the Singapore Botanic Gardens. Each of the 50-cm-long, upright inflorescences bears 15 to 20 well-arranged flowers. Each flower measures 5 cm across. The word *mas*, which means "gold" in Malay, was inspired by the brilliant yellow floral parts. A light lilac veins the lip.

***Dendrobium* Singa Star** (*Dendrobium* Fran's Twist x *Dendrobium dicuphum*). This interesting hybrid is a compact plant bearing erect to semi-erect inflorescences 40 to 45 cm in length. Each of them has 30 to 40 flowers displayed in a whorl. The natural spread of the star-shaped flower is 4.8 cm across. There are several varieties of this hybrid, but the majority of them have white floral parts that are flushed with light orchid purple except for the purple lip throat.

Dendrobium Sok Hiong Wee (_Dendrobium_ Garnet Beauty x _Dendrobium_ Premier Yusof). This is a semi-cane type hybrid that bears long arching sprays 45 to 55 cm in length, each with some 20 well-arranged flowers. The flowers are 6 cm across. Variations occur among the seedlings of this hybrid with colours of blooms ranging from deep purple to reddish orange. The sepals and petals of the clone 'Premier' are yellow at the base and gradually suffused with reddish orange to the tips; they are complemented by a broad reddish orange lip with a yellow throat. This stunning hybrid was named after the former First Lady of Singapore, Mrs. Wee Kim Wee.

Dendrobium Siti Hasmah (_Dendrobium_ Lee Ewe Boon x _Dendrobium_ Scraggy). The vigorous plant displays some 40-cm-long inflorescences with up to 30 flowers on each. Individual flowers are 4 cm across. The petals and sepals are magnolia purple with a white border. The flower is further adorned by a Scheele's green lip that is veined in magnolia purple. This orchid grows well in full sun and was named in 1981 after the wife of Dr. Mahathir, the Prime Minister of Malaysia.

Dendrobium Tien Soeharto (*Dendrobium* Noor Aishah x *Dendrobium schulleri*). This compact plant displays inflorescences 40 to 46 cm in length each bearing over 20 flowers. Individual flowers measure 4.6 cm across. The floral parts are veronese green throughout except for the lip, which is veined in cobalt violet. This orchid flowers well under full sun. It was named after the wife of the President of Indonesia, General Soeharto, on her visit to the Singapore Botanic Gardens in 1974.

Dendrobium Yuen-Peng Mc-Neice (*Dendrobium* Tan Nam Keow x *Dendrobium helix* 'Pomio Brown'). A cane-type *Dendrobium*, this robust plant produces inflorescences 50 cm in length, each with some 25 good-textured flowers. Individual flowers measure 6 cm across. The curly petals and sepals are light brown with shades of orange. This graceful hybrid was named after Lady Yuen-Peng McNeice, a former Member of the National Parks Board.

Other Hybrids

Oncidium Christine Dhanabalan (*Oncidium* Noorah x *Oncidium* Green Gold). This mule ear *Oncidium* has 35 to 45-cm-long sprays that bear some 20 well-displayed flowers. The natural spread of the good-textured flower is 4.5 cm across. The sepals and petals are yellow green and spotted in grey orange. They are complemented by a broad yellow-green lip that is spotted with greyish-red. This fine hybrid was named after the wife of Mr. S. Dhanabalan, the former Minister of National Development of Singapore.

Epilaeliocattleya Percy McNeice (*Laeliocattleya* Meadite x *Epidendrum plicatum*). The 30 to 40-cm-long inflorescences bear some 8 to 10 flowers. Each flower is 6.8 cm high and 7.7 cm across. The sepals and petals are light red with slightly darker venations. The showy lip is purple violet with a yellow throat measuring 2.5 cm wide. This lovely hybrid was named after nature lover and keen supporter of the Singapore Botanic Gardens, Sir Percy McNeice on his 90th birthday.

***Paphiopedilum* Shireen** (*Paphiopedilum glaucophyllum* x *Paphiopedilum philippinense*). This elegant primary hybrid has leaves that are 25 to 30 cm long and 6 cm wide and are dark green with light tessellations. Free-flowering and shade-loving, the plant produces hairy spikes that can grow up to 30 cm long, bearing up to 3 to 4 flowers which open one or two at a time. The flowers measure 10 cm across; the sap-green sepals are veined in dark purple; the petals are sap green gradually changing to purple towards the apex and are spotted in plum purple. The hairy sepals and petals are accompanied by a pouch-shaped lip which is light imperial purple, becoming sap-green at the base. Flowers are very attractive and long-lasting. This is the only *Paphiopedilum* hybrid produced by the Singapore Botanic Gardens and was named after the granddaughter of the Yang Di-Pertuan Agong and Permaisuri Agong in 1963.

***Spathoglottis* Primrose** (*Spathoglottis aurea* x *Spathoglottis plicata*). This is the first hybrid created in the Singapore Botanic Gardens. The 5-cm-wide flower has a light primrose colour which is flushed with pale rose purple. The long mid-lobe of the lip is bright yellow with a flush of purple pink, and the lateral-lobes and the throat are yellow with purple spots.

Ridley, H.N. (1896). *The Orchidaceae and Apostasiaceae of the Malay Peninsula.* Journal Linn. Soc. Bot. 32: 213-416

Ridley, H.N. (1907). *Materials for a Flora of the Malayan Peninsula, Vol. 1.*Singapore.

Ridley, H.N. (1924). *A Flora of the Malayan Peninsula, Vol. 4.* Ashford, Kent.

Holttum, R.E. (1953). *A Revised Flora of the Malayan Peninsula, Vol.1 Orchids.* 2nd Ed. 1957; 3rd Ed. 1964. Government Printer, Singapore.

Seidenfaden, G. and J.J. Wood (1992). *The Orchids of Peninsular Malaysia and Singapore.* Olsen & Olsen, Fredensborg.

Malayan Orchid Review (1931-1993). *A Journal of the Orchid Society of South East Asia.* Vol. 1 to 27, Singapore.

Henderson, M.R. and G.H. Addison (1956). *Malayan Orchid Hybrids.* Government Printing Office, Singapore.

Addison, G.H. (1961). *Malayan Orchid Hybrids.* First Supplement. Government Printing Office, Singapore.

Teoh, E.S. (1980). *Asian Orchids.* 2nd Ed. 1989. Times Book International.

Tan, H. and C.S. Hew (1993). *A Guide to the Orchids of Singapore.* Singapore Science Centre.

Elliott, J. (1993). *Orchid Growing in the Tropics.* Singapore. Times.

Anther Cap   The structure which covers the pollinia.

Apical   The apex of a structure.

Arachnopsis   An artificial hybrid genus produced by crossing *Arachnis* and *Trichoglottis*.

Aranda   An artificial hybrid genus produced by crossing *Arachnis* and *Vanda*.

Aranthera   An artificial hybrid genus produced by crossing *Arachnis* and *Renanthera*.

Ascocenda   An artificial hybrid genus produced by crossing *Ascocentrum* and *Vanda*.

Asymbiotic   The type of method developed by Professor Lewis Knudson for germinating orchid seeds in culture media.

Bigeneric   Describes a hybrid between two genera.

Brassidium   An artificial hybrid genus produced by crossing *Brassia* and *Oncidium*.

Cane-typed   Antelope or horn *Dendrobium* which have very long, cane-like pseudobulbs. They belong to the Spatulata section in the genus *Dendrobium*.

Christieara   An artificial hybrid genus produced by crossing *Aerides*, *Ascocentrum* and *Vanda*.

Chuanyenara   An artificial hybrid genus produced by crossing *Arachnis*, *Rhynchostylis* and *Renanthera*.

Clone   Exact copies of a plant produced by vegetative propagation or tissue culture.

Column   The structure located at the centre of the flower; it contains both the male (pollinia) and female (stigma) reproductive organs.

Culture media   Sterile media prepared for orchid seed germination and tissue culture. It contains all the major and minor elements, sugar, agar, and in some cases, plant hormones and other organic additives.

Doritaenopsis   An artificial hybrid genus produced by crossing *Doritis* and *Phalaenopsis*.

Dorsal   Back or upper dorsal sepal; refers to the single uppermost sepal.

Epilaeliocattleya   An artificial hybrid genus produced by crossing *Epidendrum*, *Laelia* and *Cattleya*.

Epiphyte   Orchids which grow on other plants for support.

Fertilisation   The fusion of the male and the female gametes. Depending on the species, it occurs several days to several months after pollination.

Gamete   A sexual cell that is able to unite with another during fertilisation.

Genus   A term used by taxonomists to indicate a certain group of orchids which share some common characteristics.

Genera   Plural form of genus.

Good-textured   Same as good substance, it is a term used to describe the thickness of the floral parts. Usually, the better the texture, the longer the life span of the flower.

Holttumara   An artificial hybrid genus produced by crossing *Arachnis, Renanthera* and *Vanda*.

Inflorescence   Flower spike.

Intermediate   Hybrids created by crossing spatulata and phalaenanthe dendrobiums. So called because their flowers are of an intermediate shape between the two sections. These hybrids are very vigorous, free-flowering, colourful, and they have longer sprays and more lasting flowers.

Laeliocattleya   An artificial hybrid genus produced by crossing *Laelia* and *Cattleya*.

Lateral-lobes   They are part of the lip and are situated at the side.

Lip   A modified petal; it is usually the most showy part of the flower. It also acts as a platform for the landing of insect pollinators.

Meristem   A group of undifferentiated cells found in young plant tissues such as apices of stems, buds, roots and young leaves.

Mid-lobe   The central portion of the lip.

Mokara   An artificial hybrid genus produced by crossing *Arachnis, Ascocentrum* and *Vanda*.

Monopodial   Orchids which grow in one direction only from the apex, as opposed to sympodial.

Mycorrhiza   A symbiotic relationship between orchid and fungus. The fungus penetrates the orchid seed and provides nutrients for seed germination.

Petals   In orchids, it refers to the inner whorl of the flower, just inside the layer of sepals. There are three petals with one modified to form the lip.

Phalaenanthe   A section belonging to the genus *Dendrobium*. Species of this section have broad petals and sepals. Some examples are *Dendrobium phalaenopsis, D. biggibum* and *D. dicuphum*. They are native to Australia's Queensland, Papua New Guinea and Indonesia.

Pseudobulb   The fleshy stem of sympodial orchids.

Pollinia   Pollen masses formed by the aggregation of individual pollen grains.

Quarter-terete   It refers to the thick leaves of this type of orchid as a result of crossing a semi-terete and a strap-leafed vandaceous species or hybrid.

Renantanda   An artificial hybrid genus produced by crossing *Renanthera* and *Vanda*.

Renanthopsis   An artificial hybrid genus produced by crossing *Renanthera* and *Paraphalaenopsis* (or *Phalaenopsis*).

Rhizome   A horizontal stem which crawls along the surface of the growing media. It bears erect pseudobulbs and roots.

Ridleyara   An artificial hybrid genus produced by crossing *Arachnis, Trichoglottis* and *Vanda*.

Rostellum   A structure which separates the stigma from the pollinia.

Seedling	A young plant which grows from seed.
Semi-terete	It refers to the fleshy leaves of this type of orchid as a result of crossing a strap-leafed and a terete vandaceous species or hybrid.
Sepals	It is the outer whorl of the flower. There are three of them in orchids just outside the petals.
Spatulata	A section belonging to the genus *Dendrobium*. It consists of plants which are also known as the antelope or the horn-type orchids, so named because their twisted petals resemble the horns of an antelope.
Species	A similar group of plants within a genus, all members being interfertile with one another.
Spur	A hollow, tube-like structure extending from the base of the lip. It contains nectar, as in *Dendrobium*.
Staminode	A sterile or abortive stamen without pollinia, as in *Paphiopedilum*.
Stigma	The sticky part of the female reproductive structure which receives the pollinia. It is situated on the side of the column facing the lip.
Strap-leaf	The flat leathery, strap like leaves of vandaceous orchids.
Substance	A term used to describe the thickness of the floral parts. Usually, the better the substance, the longer the life span of the flower.
Sympodial	Orchids which grow by producing new shoots through horizontal stems or rhizomes.
Tepals	Petals and sepals which look alike.
Terete	Pencil-like fleshy leaves of vandaceous orchids, as in *Vanda teres* and *Paraphalaenopsis* species.
Terrestrial	Orchids which grow on the ground.
Vandaceous	The group of monopodial orchids which consists of some of the most showy species of Asia. They include genera such as *Aerides, Arachnis, Renanthera, Rhynchostylis* and *Vanda*.
Vandaenopsis	An artificial hybrid genus produced by crossing *Phalaenopsis* (or *Paraphalaenopsis*) and *Vanda*.
Variety	A clone of a species or hybrid which is different from the others.
Vascostylis	An artificial hybrid genus produced by crossing *Ascocentrum, Rhynchostylis* and *Vanda*.
Velamen	A layer (or layers) of dead cells situated on the surface of epiphytic orchid roots. It is known to function as a sponge to absorb water during wet periods and release it slowly during the dry intervals.
VIP orchids	Orchids named after VIPs during their visit to the Singapore Botanic Gardens.

INDEX

Aerides lawrenceae Rchb.f. — 47
Aerides houlettiana Rchb.f — 48
Aerides quinquevulnera — 48
Aeridovanda Jehan El Sadat — 106
Alphonso, A. G. — 24
American Orchid Society — 13
Anderson, J. W. — 16
Angraecum eburneum Bory — 84
Angraecum leonis (Rchb.f.) Veitch — 85
Angraecum sesquipedale Thou. — 85
Anoectochilus albolineatus Par. & Rchb.f. — 36
Arachnis flosaeris (L.) Rchb.f. — 49
Arachnis hookeriana (Rchb.f.) Rchb.f. — 36
Arachnis Ishbel — 106
Arachnis Maggie Oei — 19
Arachnoglottis Brown Bars — 107
Arachnopsis Eric Holttum — 107
Aranda Belzonica — 108
Aranda Bertha Braga — 108
Aranda Deborah — 109
Aranda Eric Mekie — 109
Aranda Grandeur — 110
Aranda Hilda Galistan — 110
Aranda How Yee Peng — 24
Aranda Majula — 13,111
Aranda Nancy O'Neil — 111
Aranda Noorah Alsagoff — 26
Aranda Peter Ewart — 112
Aranthera Anne Black — 112
Aranthera Dainty — 113
Aranthera James Storie — 113
Aranthera Mohamed Haniff — 20
Artificial pollination — 34
Arundina graminifolia (D. Don) Hochr. — 37
Ascocenda Iris Harris — 114
Ascocenda Singa Chiba — 114
Asymbiotic orchid seed germination — 17
Black, Lady — 23
Black, Sir Robert — 23
Brassavola nodosa (L.) Lindl. — 88
Breeding goals — 99
Breeding programme — 24,97
Bulbophyllum barbigerum Lindl. — 86
Bulbophyllum blepharistes Rchb.f. — 50
Bulbophyllum gusdorfii J. J. Sm. — 50
Bulbophyllum lobbii Lindl. — 51

Bulbophyllum medusae (Lindl.) Rchb.f. — 35
Bulbophyllum vaginatum (Lindl.) Rchb.f. — 32,38
Burgeff, H. — 17
Burkill, H.M. — 23
Burkill, I.H. — 16
Calanthe Dominyi — 17
Calanthe vestita Lindl. — 51
Cantley, N. — 15
Carr, C.E. — 20
Catasetum pileatum Rchb.f. — 88
Catasetum saccatum Lindl. — 89
Caularthron bicornutum (Hook.) Schultes — 90
Christieara Ramiah — 115
Chuanyenara Mei-Tsung — 115
Cleisostoma lanatum (Lindl.) ex G. Don. — 52
Climbers — 33
Coelogyne asperata Lindl. — 52
Coelogyne mayeriana Rchb.f. — 39
Coelogyne zuriwetzii Carr — 53
Cold House — 27,34
Column — 11
Conservation — 34
Corymborkis veratrifolium (Reinw.) Bl. — 39
Curtis, C. — 16
Cycnoches pentadactylon Lindl. — 87
Cymbidium ensifolium (L.) Sw. — 53
Cyrtorchis arcuata (Lindl.) Schltr. — 86
Dendrobium anosmum Lindl. — 54
Dendrobium Asean Beauty — 130
Dendrobium chrysotoxum Lindl. — 54
Dendrobium cretaceum Lindl. — 55
Dendrobium crumenatum Sw. — 40
Dendrobium dearei Rchb.f. — 55
Dendrobium De Klerk — 131
Dendrobium Elizabeth — 131
Dendrobium farmeri Paxt. — 56
Dendrobium findlayanum Parish & Rchb.f. — 56
Dendrobium formosum Roxb. ex Lindl. — 57
Dendrobium Gloria Lim — 132
Dendrobium Helen Park — 18
Dendrobium helix P. J. Cribb — 57
Dendrobium Iwen Tan — 132
Dendrobium Jane Denny — 133
Dendrobium John Nauen — 133
Dendrobium Khunying Boonruen — 134
Dendrobium lasianthera J.J. Sm. — 58

Dendrobium leonis (Lindl.) Rchb.f. — 40
Dendrobium lineale Rolfe — 58
Dendrobium Margaret Thatcher — 134
Dendrobium Masako Kotaishi Hidenka — 135
Dendrobium Michiko — 136
Dendrobium moschatum (Buch. Ham.) — 59
Dendrobium National Parks — 136
Dendrobium nindii W. Hill — 59
Dendrobium Premier Yusof — 137
Dendrobium Ria — 137
Dendrobium Richard Hale — 138
Dendrobium Ryzhkova — 138
Dendrobium Saleha — 139
Dendrobium secundum (Bl.) Lindl. — 41
Dendrobium Singa Dear Mary — 139
Dendrobium Singa Mas — 140
Dendrobium Singa Star — 140
Dendrobium Siti Hasmah — 141
Dendrobium smillieae F. Muell. — 60
Dendrobium Sok Hiong Wee — 141
Dendrobium spectabile (Bl.) Miq. — 61
Dendrobium stratiotes Rchb.f. — 61
Dendrobium tangerinum P.J. Cribb — 62
Dendrobium taurinum Lindl. — 62
Dendrobium Tay Swee Keng — 25
Dendrobium Tien Soeharto — 142
Dendrobium Yuen-Peng McNeice — 142
Dominy, J. — 17
Doritaenopsis Elizabeth Waldheim — 116
Doritis pulcherrima Lindl. — 63
Elliot, J. — 7
Encyclia fragrans (Sw.) Lemee. — 90
Epidendroideae — 31
Epidendrum ibaguense H.B.K. — 91
Epilaeliocattleya Percy McNeice — 143
Epiphytic orchids — 32
Eria hyacinthoides (Bl.) Lindl. — 41
Eria multiflora (Bl.) Lindl. — 64
Eria javanica (Sw.) Bl. — 42
Eria pubescens (Hook.) Steud — 64
Eria xanthocheila Ridl. — 65
Euanthe sanderiana (Rchb.f.) Schltr. — 65
Eulophia andamanensis Rchb.f. — 66
Eulophia spectabilis (Dennst.) Suresh — 42
Flickingeria comata (Bl.) Hawkes — 66
Galistan, E. — 20

Gardens Catalogue 16
Geesinkorchis alaticallosa de Vogel 67
Geodorum citrinum Jacks. 67
Gongora quinquenervis Ruiz & Pavon 91
Geographical distribution 33
Grammatophyllum speciosum Bl. 43
Habenaria rhodocheila Hance. 68
Henderson, M. R. 22
Herbarium 21
Holttum, R. E. 17,18,20,21,22,97,100,104
Holttumara Cochineal 7,116
Hybridisation 99
Ionopsis utricularioides (Sw.) Lindl. 92
Ishak, Yusof 24
Jewel orchids 33
Joaquim, Agnes 16
Knudson, L. 18,100
Landscaping 97
Laycock, J. 18
Lewis, G. 24
Liparis maingayi (Hook.f.) Ridl. 68
Malayan Orchid Review 6,20
Malayan Orchid Society 20
Micropropagation 25
Monopodials 9
Murton, H. J. 15
Mycorrhiza 11
National Flower of Singapore 9,16
National Orchid Garden 26,27
National Parks Board 26,27
Nephelaphyllum pulchrum Bl. 32,44
Oeceoclades saundersiana
  (Rchb.f.) Garay & Taylor 83
Oncidium Christine Dhanabalan 143
Oncidium Goldiana 19
Oncidium lanceanum Lindl. 93
Oncidium sphacelatum Lindl. 93
Orchid Enclosure 6
Orchid House 15
Orchid industry 25
Orchid Society of South East Asia 12,20
Orchidarium 26
Paphiopedilum barbatum (Lindl.) Pfitz. 69
Paphiopedilum lowii (Lindl.) Stein 69
Paphiopedilum Shireen 144
Papilionanthe hookeriana (Rchb.f.) Schltr. 70

Papilionanthe teres (Roxb.) Schltr. 70
Paraphalaenopsis denevei J.J.Sm. 72
Paraphalaenopsis labukensis Lam, Chan & Shim 72
Penang Botanic Gardens 16
Peristeria elata Hook. 94
Pigeon Orchid 40
Phaius tankervilleae (Banks ex l'Heritier) Bl. 44
Phalaenopsis amabilis (L.) Blume 73
Phalaenopsis amboinensis J.J.Sm. 73
Phalaenopsis Barbara Bush 117
Phalaenopsis lueddemanniana Rchb.f. 74
Phalaenopsis schilleriana Rchb.f. 74
Phalaenopsis stuartiana Rchb.f. 75
Phalaenopsis violacea Witte 75
Plocoglottis javanica Bl. 45
Pollinators 100
Pollinia 11,100
Potted plants 101
Pseudobulbs 9
Purseglove, J. W. 23
Registration 13
Renantanda Akihito 118
Renantanda Hannelore Schmidt 118
Renantanda Jane McNeill 24,105
Renantanda Keating 119
Renantanda Mary Robinson 120
Renantanda Prince Norodom Sihanouk 120
Renanthera bella J.J. Wood 76
Renanthera philippinensis Ames & Quis. 76
Renanthera Rattanakosin 121
Renanthopsis Dhanabalan 121
Reproductive organs 9
Rhyncholaelia digbyana (Lindl.) Schltr. 94
Rhynchostylis gigantea (Lindl.) Ridl. 77
Rhynchostylis retusa (L.) Bl. 77
Ridley, H. N. 15
Ridleyara Fascad 122
Rostellum 11
Royal Horticultural Society 13
Sander's List of Orchid Hybrids 13
Saprophytes 11
Seed germination 11,100
Seeds 11,100
Sophronites cernua Lindl. 95
Spathoglottis affinis de Vriese 78
Spathoglottis Parsons Junior 145

Spathoglottis plicata Bl. 45
Spathoglottis Primrose 145
Spathoglottis vanoverberghii 78
Stigma 11
Stud plants 24,99
Symbiotic fungus 11,17
Sympodials 9
Taeniophyllum obtusum Bl. 46
Tan, H. S. 22
Tan, J. H. 2
Tan, Kiat W. 3,25
Teoh, E. S. 6
Terrestrial orchids 32
The 4th World Orchid Conference 24
The RHS Orchid Information System 13
Thrixspermum amplexicaule (Bl.) Rchb. F. 46
Tissue culture 25
Trichoglottis loheriana (Kranzl.) L.O. Wms. 79
Trichoglottis philippinensis Lindl. 79
Trigonidium egertonianum Batem. ex Lindl. 95
Vanda Bellasan 123
Vanda dearei Rchb.f. 80
Vanda Farah Pahlavi 123
Vanda insignis Bl. 80
Vanda Memoria Alex Donald 124
Vanda Miss Joaquim 16,71
Vanda Norbert Alphonso 125
Vanda Prolific 2,3,126
Vanda Rubella 126
Vanda Sanada Kuma 127
Vanda Singa Joaquim Centenary 127
Vanda sumatrana Schltr. 81
Vanda Tan Chay Yan 22
Vanda tricolor Lindl. 81
Vanda Wong Poh Nee 128
Vandaenopsis Leo Tan 129
Vandaenopsis Sisir 128
Vandopsis gigantea (Lindl.) Pfitz. 82
Vandopsis warocqueana Schltr. 82
Vanilla 33
Velamen 11
VIP orchid 23
World War II 18
Yam, T.W. 96,152

Acknowledgements

I would like to take this opportunity to thank Dr. Tan Wee Kiat, Executive Director of the National Parks Board, for the privilege of this challenging assignment and for his guidance throughout the project.

I would like to thank Mr. John Tan Jiew Hoe for generously sponsoring the production of the book. As a gesture of appreciation, this book is dedicated to Mr. Tan Hoon Siang, John's father and the breeder of the renowned Vanda Tan Chay Yan.

I am indebted to many others who have helped in the project: Miss Peggy Tan for editing, encouragement, patience and many sessions of fruitful discussion; Drs. Chin See Chung, Foong Thai Woo, Leong Chee Chiew and Miss Jean Khoo for useful comments on the first draft; Mrs. Bonnie Tinsley and Mr. James Teng for editing; Mr. Eng Siak Loy and Miss Chan Choy Har for the illustrations; Miss Eileen Tay and Miss Chan Hui San for putting all the information together in the present form; Mrs. Maureen Lim - Desouza for coordination; Mr. Peyton Coffin for initiating the project; Miss Joyce Teo and Miss Alison Ng for general assistance; Miss Whang Lay Kheng and Miss Goh Siew Sim for looking after the beautiful orchids in our living collection.

Finally, I thank my wife Pauline and my daughters, Grace and Amy, for the support and joy they provided throughout the preparation of this book.

Dr. Yam Tim Wing